HOW TO WIN AT
CASINO GAMBLING

THIS IS A CARLTON BOOK

Copyright © Carlton Books Limited 1996

First published in 1996 by Carlton Books Limited

10 9 8 7 6 5 4 3 2 1

A CIP catalogue record for this book is available from the British Library

Photos courtesy of Casino Player magazine, the world's largest publication for gaming enthusiasts. All photos by Rick Greco, Casino Player Photo Editor. Casino Player, 8025 Black Horse Pike, Suite 470, West Atlantic City, NJ 08232 USA Tel: 800 846 7529 Fax: 609 645 1661

ISBN 0 7475 2698 2

Printed and bound in Spain

Carlton Books Limited
20 St Anne's Court
Wardour Street
London W1V 3AW

HOW TO WIN AT CASINO GAMBLING

ROGER GROS
Senior Editor of *Casino Player* magazine

CARLTON

CONTENTS

INTRODUCTION

What is it that makes gambling so pervasive in human nature? Every choice you make in life is a gamble. When you are finally old enough to make your own choices, you gamble with your future with every decision you make. What college should you attend? What profession should you enter? Should you get married and who should you marry? All these questions are the spice of which life is made. And they are all gambles.

The reason so many people enjoy gambling is because it feels familiar. The choices you make each day in real life are easily translated into the choices you make in the casino. You use many of the same strategies to make choices in real life as you do when you're gambling in the casino. Some of the assumptions you make in the casino cannot be translated to real life, however. And that's where gambling and real life diverge.

Luck is, of course, the essential element in casino gambling. Sure, you can mitigate that factor by understanding the odds and the most favorable ways to play the games, but you can't eliminate it.

The same goes for life. Luck plays an enormous role in how your life is played out. You can get a good education and be totally prepared for your career, but if you don't meet that one key person in your professional life, or you don't get an unexpected break, you may only be moderately successful, rather than soar into the rarefied heights of your chosen profession.

Unlike gambling, where the decisions on the various games will break even over the long run, you can't depend upon real life to "even up". Bad luck can dog an individual his entire life, for reasons unknown to anyone except for a higher being. Don't expect things to turn around because you are due for a break. You have to make your own breaks.

CHANGING YOUR LUCK

When you're gambling and losing, the natural inclination is to try to do something to win. That can often be the worst strategy. By continuing to gamble, you're risking more of your bankroll, and you have a greater than average chance of losing. Why? Because now you're playing with "scared money"—that is, money that you never planned to risk, but now believe you must. Because it's more than you planned to risk, your decisions will often be suspect, and you will play more emotionally than rationally and expose yourself to some very harsh life-lessons.

The same is true in life. If things aren't going well for you on a particular project, for instance, you can get angry. Anger never makes it better, it can only make things worse. And when you get angry, emotional, exasperated or you feel that you simply don't care, you are going to lose…in real life or while gambling.

It doesn't matter how much time or money you've invested, either. If you're playing blackjack, and you have to make a difficult decision, don't think about how much money you've lost already. It doesn't matter, and it certainly won't affect whether you win or lose that particular hand. If it affects how you play, you're in bad shape.

Let's go back to the stock market for a real-life situation. Suppose you purchased stock in a particular company for $10,000. Now suppose that company suffered some downturns that no one anticipated, bringing your stock down to $5,000. But another investor is willing to pay you $8,000 for that stock. You don't want to take that offer because you believe you'll be losing $2,000. But if you accept his offer, you'd actually be picking up $3,000. It doesn't matter what you paid for the stock initially, it only matters what it's worth at the moment you get the offer. Make the decision on that basis, not on past events.

6

PLAYING THE GAME

Poker players understand that the secret to success is just that…a secret! Successful poker players don't reveal their hands unless they absolutely have to at the end of the game. Players who talk about their losing hand, or expose a winning hand when they don't have to, are not likely to be winners for very long.

By exposing or discussing your hands unnecessarily, you are revealing your strategies. And that gives your opponents crucial hints about your thought processes and tactics.

The same is true in real life. People who talk about their most intimate secrets give others information that they may be able to use in future situations. People make these revelations because they want to be friendly, but you can still be friendly without revealing information that may be dangerous later on. Instead of talking about your own strategies, ask other people about themselves. They'll think you are simply taking an interest in their life, and be glad to talk about themselves. Most people, whether they are potential competitors or not, are flattered to be asked about their opinions. Remember their answers. You may be able to use them in a future encounter.

But when those future encounters occur and you get the upper hand, don't try to rub it in. Be gracious in victory and in defeat. You don't want to make enemies. It's difficult enough to get the advantage. If you have to worry about someone trying to "get even", you'll further complicate your life…or your gambling.

Even if you've been humiliated by an opponent, don't try to get even yourself. In almost every situation, some people are going to get the better of others. That's life, and that's gambling. Move on, and play for the next opportunity. If you're as gracious a winner as you are a loser, no one will feel the need to "get even" with you.

Remember Murphy's Law: everything that can possibly go wrong, will go wrong. The most obnoxious and least knowledgeable player can sometimes be the luckiest. It's not right, but it happens. And it happens more often than we'd like to believe.

In real life, injustices occur every day. If you spent hours fretting about every event that was beyond your control, you'd go crazy. It's a waste of time, energy, and money. Leave those injustices behind and prepare for better days.

Gambling and life have many similarities. That's why people enjoy casinos so much. But like many things in life, gambling also holds many risks and rewards. By understanding the stakes, you can make the most of your life and your gambling.

The book we've put together here is a general guide to casino gambling, in its most basic form. I've indicated in most cases where the games get more complicated, but do not go into detail in these areas since it is rarely necessary unless you intend to make casino gambling a true vocation.

While my experience is strictly with the casinos of North America, I've tried to make all the information applicable to casinos around the world. Where there are differences, I have made notations in the text.

Certainly, there are some major differences between European casinos and those in the United States, but the games are essentially the same. The procedures and advice offered in this book should be applicable to all situations.

The same is true of the way money is handled in the book. Although the only currency used throughout the book is US Dollars the advice remains the same. This should certainly be the perfect gambling companion for you, whichever country you choose to play in and whichever currency you choose to use.

At the end of every chapter, you'll find a section entitled "The Systems Approach." This is designed to give you a real-life feel about how some people approach casino gambling. Some of the stories in this section are designed to give you tips about specific ways to play, while others are warnings of some of gaming's most attractive pitfalls. In any case, I hope you'll find this section enlightening.

And finally, to avoid being labelled a chauvinist, I'd like to make one disclaimer. In all instances when I refer to gamblers or casino employees, I use the masculine gender. This is not to say that all gamblers, dealers or pit bosses are male. It is only a device I use for simplicity, rather than have to resort to the he/she or him/her approach.

I hope you enjoy this book, but most of all, I hope it allows you to enjoy casino gambling as I do. But please, only gamble what you can afford, and if you find it entertaining–and sometimes profitable–we may rub elbows someday at the baccarat tables.

CHAPTER 1

CASINO PSYCHOLOGY

I THINK, THEREFORE I GAMBLE

Think of casino executives as skilled psychologists who understand how to motivate gamblers. If you understand the casino's point of view, you have an opportunity to enhance your chances of winning and your enjoyment of the casino experience.

Gambling is the great equalizer. Sure, there is a definite class system in place in casinos around the world, but winning and losing affects everyone equally. While the levels of gains or losses vary between the nickel slot machine and the private baccarat or chemin de fer tables, the impact is usually similar. Winning brings excitement and exhilaration, losing brings disappointment and despair.

Casinos are the temples of gambling. From the small closets and back rooms of illegal gambling dens to today's glittering entertainment palaces, casinos are generally where gamblers go to experience the thrill of placing their hard-earned money on the line.

But let's not begin with any illusions. Gambling is a game for losers, for there is no way to beat the casino. The built-in house advantage at every casino game will grind down even the most experienced player in the long run. Those who have discovered a winning "system" are generally experiencing short-term deviations from the long-term law of averages.

But short-term is what most people play, so the chances of winning in a casino are much better than winning a lottery, a bingo game or a church raffle. By learning the games and understanding how to reduce the house edge to its lowest possible percentage, you can give yourself a fighting chance, and may even arrive home a winner. You can make the most of your casino experience by knowing what games to play and how to play them.

CASINO CULTURE

Casinos of the past were rather modest affairs with just a few table games in small rooms. Their legal status varied wildly throughout the years, but today, some form of legal casino gambling is offered in 28 of the 50 United States.

Whether they are Indian casinos, riverboats, dockside or land-based, there is a casino within a three hour drive of three-quarters of the American population. It is therefore not necessary for the serious player to visit any of the illegal casinos that still exist in the big cities of the United States.

The major casino gaming activity in the US today is centered in Nevada and Atlantic City. Spectacular casino hotels are the current preferred choice in adult entertainment. While the resorts offer everything from theme parks, spas and luxurious suites to superstar entertainment, championship sporting events and shopping, the main focus remains on gambling in the casino.

European resorts like Monaco in France, Spain's Gold Coast and Germany's Baden-Baden offer different kinds of casino experiences, but they all rely on one thing: the ability of their clients to play...and lose.

The American-style casino is different from the European casino. In most cases, the European casinos are reserved for the middle and upper classes, with entry fees, memberships or location serving as an effective barrier to those who either can't afford to join or aren't acceptable as members.

In the US, most casinos are open to everyone, with few restrictions on participation outside of age or criminal background. American casinos, like many aspects of the American culture, are aimed at the masses.

All gaming resorts make the lion's share of their money from the casino, so it is important to them that customers play in their casino as long as possible. Casino executives understand that the longer people play, the more likely they are to lose. Remember, in the short-term, you can profit from deviations from the law of averages, but the longer you play, the more vulnerable you are to the house edge.

To get you into the casino in a gaming resort that features other entertainment amenities, the house employs a variety of tools. The regulations vary from jurisdiction to jurisdiction, so many of these methods do not apply, but in general, the idea is to get the customer into the casino and keep them there as long as possible.

In Nevada, you can't walk anywhere in a hotel without walking through the casino. Even when you're checking in, you usually have to walk through the slot machines to get to the front desk. The friendly din of the slot machines is audible whenever you leave your room, encouraging you to slip a few coins into the machine and yank the arm just in case it's your lucky day.

In the past, many casinos decorated their sleeping rooms in garish colors and busy designs. This was supposed to make

the guest restless and encourage them to return to the casino. You'll notice that televisions in casino rooms don't sport a wide variety of channels and in most cases, there are no "minibars", so people are forced to leave their rooms in search of a drink.

Even if you're eating in a casino restaurant, you're still not insulated from the games. Keno runners will skip from table to table accepting bets for the next keno game. The keno numbers can be seen from every vantage point in the hotel. Some casinos have designed special slot machines that will let you eat while you play in a bid to maximize business.

Alcohol plays a large role in keeping you in the casino. Cocktail waitresses circulate frequently through the tables and the slots to ply the players with free drinks. Alcohol greases the casino's cash stream. Even when you want to take a break, casino taverns have "bar-top" video poker machines embedded in the bar, that constantly flash their appealing message. It's difficult to sit still and resist the temptation to try your luck.

Many casinos pump extra levels of oxygen into their ventilation systems, which gives players a feeling of well-being, making them feel "lucky" and perhaps increase their

wagers. However, casino executives defend this practice by saying they are just increasing the fresh air flow.

Don't expect to see any clocks in a casino. The executives want you to lose track of time and not know—or care—whether it's night or day. Windows were never originally included in casino design, but that concept is beginning to change now that most casinos are located in resort areas that have spectacular vistas.

Today's casinos take advantage of those great views so that when you sit at a gaming table or slot machine, you can partake in the surroundings. You can then truly return home with tales of the beautiful scenery, even if you never left the casino.

CASINO CONNECTION

Let's take a trip through a mythical casino. As we drive up to the glittering building, we enter the porte-cochère, where a valet hustles up to the car and welcomes us to the resort. We approach the doors and as they swing open, they reveal the colorful, noisy and exciting casino. Lights are flashing, bells are ringing and people are chattering about the action unfolding before them. It's a gateway into a new world.

The bright lights and constant action are meant to draw us into the depths of the casino. Watch the slot machines near the entrance. Many slot experts theorize that casino executives place the higher paying machines at the casino entrance to give the impression that people are winning throughout the whole establishment.

While no slot executive has ever admitted to subscribing to that theory, many players assume it is true and will only play at machines near the entrance.

Conversely, machines near the coin cashier (the "cage") are supposedly tighter, and pay out less than other machines throughout the casino. The theory here, is that players heading to the cage will be captured on the way, and since it may be the last chance the casino has to get their money, the house had better make the most of it.

Again, executive corroboration of this method has rarely, if ever, been obtained.

We resist the high-paying entrance slots and proceed to the jaws of the casino. As we plunge further into its depths, we are engulfed by the various wagering options. The machines are everywhere, of course, each beckoning with different themes, colors and payoffs.

Blackjack dealers busily distribute the cards, while welcoming new players with broad smiles. Roulette dealers sweep the layouts clean of losing bets and push out a veritable mountain of chips to the winners. Players of the most exciting of all games, craps, bellow their approval when the "shooter" makes his point.

But it is the impersonal slot machine that makes its presence most felt. The modern slot machine is no longer simply the one-armed bandit. Compared to its predecessors, the new slots are seductresses, luring their players with a variety of ploys. Sounds drift from nearly every machine, whether being played or not. Appealing squeaks, squawks and pleasant voices vie for the attention of passers-by. Even the deaf would have a hard time ignoring these machines, for colorful glass, shiny brass and state-of-the-art graphics on the screens of the devices complete the job the noises have only begun. The latest machines even glow when a jackpot is hit.

Further on, the sports and race book features floor-to-ceiling television screens, private betting areas and rows of seats that enable customers to stay in touch with sporting events around the world. When the American National Football League is in season, the area constantly erupts as bettors react to different plays on the various screens.

Show bands in the adjacent lounges add to the general cacophony of the casino, transporting players to yet another level of fantasy. The dress code in most casinos is decidedly casual these days, but on special events—superstar entertainment or a boxing championship—elegantly dressed men and women who pass through at any hour of the day or night, just adding to the allure of the casino gaming experience.

As we reach the secluded rear of the casino, the action really heats up. The high limit slot machines—including a couple of $500 jobs—are set aside by themselves, with the players getting personalized treatment that may include a back massage, warm towels or a meal delivered to the machines. These are the "high rollers" of the slot world, and very valuable to any casino.

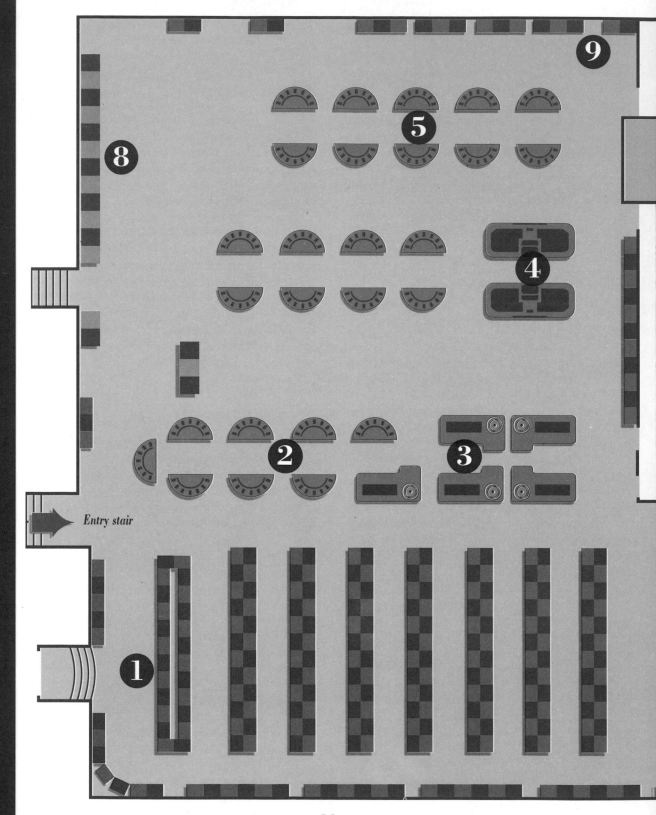

Entry stair

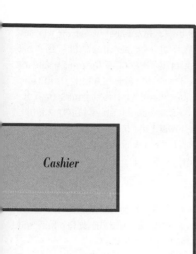

Cashier

Bar and storage area

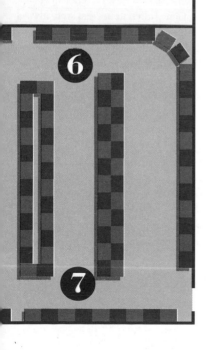

CASINO LAYOUT

1 Upon entering the casino, patrons will be faced with a wall of slot machines. Since the slots will be visible from outside the casino, casino executives may place the higher paying slots near the door so that hotel guests may see players winning and collecting jackpots. A linked progressive slot carousel will include a high jackpot, with flashing lights and a digital display with spinning numbers showing the jackpot progressing upward.

2 The blackjack tables will be the first to open, and will have the most unfavorable rules in the casino because they are the most convenient.

3 The roulette tables may be hard to find because they are not very popular and don't contribute a major portion to the casino's bottom line.

4 The same is also true of the craps tables so you'll have to search those out as well.

5 The blackjack tables at the back of the casino; they're either a low denomination that doesn't contribute a great deal to the casino revenue or give a more favorable payback.

6 Most casinos will scatter their favorable machines throughout the casino, so you're just as apt to find a high paying machine in the back of the Casino as in the front. The lower denomination machines are often the most difficult to find.

7 You should expect to search the casino floor for the nickel machines.

8 The video poker machines are gathered in a central location. In casinos in jurisdictions with savvy gamblers, such as Las Vegas or Atlantic City, there would be more video poker machines, because your decisions can effect how much money you win.

9 The machines by the cashier are most likely the "tightest" machines in the house. The theory is that players are taking their winnings to the cashier and those machines are the last chance to get that money back. Players with weak wills may decide to try their luck before cashing out.

The "premium" tables are located in the baccarat pit. Half-a-dozen blackjack tables cater to the elite of the gaming world. Minimums start at $100 and head up sharply. The elegant game of baccarat, where minimums starts at $25 and maximums can soar to more than $1 million, often loses its charm when players' losses mount, turning them surly and sullen. A "French" roulette wheel—a table with simply a single "0" instead of the less favorable "00"—waits for the knowledgeable high roller to try his luck.

Consider a casino like you would a supermarket. You know that you have to go to the back of the store to buy milk. Everyone needs milk, and it is often priced as a loss-leader to get the customers in the door. The supermarket executives want you to walk by all the high-profit items to get to that milk so you'll buy other items on impulse.

The same is true in a casino. The best-paying slot machines are usually difficult to find. You have to hunt for them, and many players will simply give up and play the machine that is the most convenient. This machine is most likely one of the lowest paying machines in the house.

The same tactics apply for table games. What do you see when you first enter the table-game area? The Big Six wheel, the money wheel, or the wheel of fortune, whatever it's called in that casino, it is there click-clacking its illusory message. The odds are so terrible for this game, that the casino generally keeps half the money played on this table. But walk down the aisle toward the back of the casino, and you may find a very favorable blackjack table that has rules that almost favor the player.

Casino executives consider themselves successful when they can convince players to leave their inhibitions at the door, suspend their perception of time, and create a new and exciting reality—even if it is a fantasy.

THAT WINNING ATTITUDE

People have varying reasons for gambling. For most people, it's the excitement of the game, the escape from day-to-day reality, and the thrill of a potential cash windfall. It's called "casino entertainment" these days because many people are willing to accept a reasonable loss in exchange for a few hours of action at the machines or the tables.

The loss is the price for that excitement, not unlike the price you'd pay for a ticket at a sporting event. The thing that makes casino entertainment different is that you always have the chance to get that excitement and still come out a winner. It's a version of the "something for nothing" factor, which could be a sub-plot to the American Dream.

Since luck is involved in almost every gaming decision, it's important to go into the games with the right attitude. While some people are willing to accept a reasonable loss for a reasonable amount of gambling time, it would be a mistake to begin your playing session by writing off your bankroll.

Positive thinking works wonders in real life, so there's no reason it can't be successfully utilized in the casino environment. Other people travel to a casino with one goal: to win. Entertainment doesn't enter into their thought process, their only satisfaction will come from beating the house. More often than not, these types of players go home disappointed, and often bitter, about their casino experience. While many people with this mindset have prepared for their casino challenge by studying and practicing, reality very rarely mirrors the ideal conditions they anticipated during their practice sessions. Gambling near a person of this sort can sometimes be unpleasant, as they often take a hostile attitude towards casino personnel and other players.

This is not to say you shouldn't play to win. It's simply that the expectation to win every time is not realistic, given the hefty casino advantage in almost every game.

GETTING STARTED

Casinos can be imposing, overwhelming places. Other, more experienced players can often make a newcomer feel intimidated and unwelcome. These situations can easily be avoided by knowing the basics of casino etiquette.

For many new players, the slot machines are the most familiar and the least threatening of all the games in a casino. It's easy to buy some coins and sit for hours in front of one machine pumping in the money. In fact, most modern slot machines now have bill acceptors that make coins and any contact with a "change person" (a casino employee who sells rolls of coins or tokens) obsolete.

The bill acceptors will take any denomination of bill from $1 to $20 and above. After inserting the bill, the machines will most likely register credits on the machine rather than spit out the corresponding number of coins or tokens. If you prefer to play with coins, however, it's simply a matter of hitting the "cash out" button, that will spill the coins into the payout tray of the slot machine.

Choosing the slot machine to play is generally as simple as deciding what denomination you want to play. Remember two things: the larger the denomination, the larger the payout to the player; slot machines are programmed to win.

Casino executives love slot machines, which is a good reason why you should not. In the past 20 years, the percentage of casino revenue derived by slot machines have changed places with table games. It used to be that the table games accounted for over 60 percent of casino revenue. Slot machines were provided for their entertainment value and aimed at the wives of the table game players.

Things began to change as table game players got older, and began to disappear. The newer casino customers weren't comfortable with table games, but did respond to the more modern and recognizable slot machines. With ATM machines, computers and televisions an ingrained part of our culture, slot machines became the choice of many of the casinos' younger customers.

Today, slot machines account for over 60 percent of casino revenue. In some jurisdictions, it's even higher. Table games, meanwhile, have undergone a dramatic decline in interest. Players continue to disappear, and developing new table game players is costly for the casinos, and not as profitable as simply letting them find their way to the slot machines.

Because most table games offer a house edge that is dramatically less than most slot machines, casino executives don't lose any sleep over players moving from tables to slots.

Even slot machines that have good payback percentages (the ratio of money returned to the player to the money played) generally pay back far less than a player can achieve by playing intelligently at a craps table, a blackjack game or in the baccarat pit. Even American roulette ranks near the top of the best slot machine payback.

Yes, slot machines are fun and non-intimidating, but they also take your money faster than any major table game. Casinos are gathering places. By sitting in front of a slot machine the entire day, you miss out on the social interaction that can be so rewarding in the casino. Break down the barriers and give table games a try.

After reading this book, you'll understand the basics of each game, and you'll at least have the knowledge of what bets are good to make, what bets are longshots with unacceptable house edges, and what bets the casino executives don't want you to know about.

So let's meander over to the table games and jump right in. The water's fine!

CASINO REVENUES

TABLE GAMES Vs SLOT MACHINES		
	1975	1995
Table Games	65%	35%
Slot Machines	35%	65%

BUYING TIME

Chips are the currency of the casino. Although a few casinos in Nevada still allow you to bet with real money, most casinos require you to exchange your money for chips.

However, there's another psychological casino trick at work here. Be aware that chips are just like money. You can get up from any table and carry your chips over to the casino cage and exchange them for money. The casino wants you to treat the chips like play money. That's why they are generally very colorful and fun to play with while you're considering your next move. Remember, chips are money, and when you bet them you should visualize a stack of cash. Chips are fantasy, cash is reality.

Once you realize that little axiom, getting started is rather easy. At Nevada and European casinos, you are permitted to go to the cage to exchange your money for chips.

In many other jurisdictions, you must "buy in" (exchange your cash for chips) at the gaming tables. That doesn't necessarily mean you have to play at that specific table, but you can only buy the chips at the tables.

When you present your cash buy-in to the dealer, don't put it in a betting area. Make sure that he understands that you want to exchange your cash for chips.

Once you've decided what game to play, pay attention to the table minimums and maximums. Generally, tables have a sign that indicate that information, as well as a series of reminders about the special rules in effect at that table or in that casino.

If you only have $100 to gamble, you don't want to sit down at a table that requires a $25 minimum bet. As you'll see in the next chapter, you need to consider your bankroll in making a determination about the minimum bet. And that decision will vary depending upon the game you eventually choose to play.

But by choosing to play table games, you've already got a leg up on the slot players who must battle often prohibitive odds to leave as winners. Give yourself a chance, play the tables.

THE SYSTEMS APPROACH

KNOWING THE SCORE

Let's get something straight right from the beginning. The more money the casinos can extract from the pockets of their players, the more money they are going to make. It's that simple.

So the basic principle is that the more money you can keep in your pocket, or return to your pocket after playing, the more money you are going to take home.

Casinos have come up with a new innovation for slot machines that seemingly makes it easier for them to get that money out of your pocket and into the machines. It's called a "bill acceptor". By providing a way for you to preload the machines with cash is mainly a method of pumping up profits. They don't have to hire change persons, they handle fewer coins, and they get greater play because you spend more time on the machine.

What casinos have ignored, or simply overlooked, is that bill acceptors—along with the credit meters on modern machines—offer an important and previously missing element: a way to keep score.

Table-game players are able to track their bankrolls, because they have their chips in front of them at all times. They know how much they cashed in for and can determine how much they have at any time, so they can determine their wins or losses.

Until recently, slot players haven't been able to keep score, unless you kept track by the number of the discarded coin wrappers on the floor around the machine.

Bill acceptors can make all the difference. Decide ahead of time on your buy-in, whether it's what you have budgeted to play for the entire session, or what you've allocated for a particular machine. Pre-load the machine with the whole amount. Since you don't have to use coins, there's no reason to start with part of what you're willing to risk then dig for more if your initial buy-in is lost. When you use the bill acceptor, the credit meter shows you your exact status at any instant. The only math you have to do is convert the number of coins to dollars (or your native currency).

Pre-loading the machine with your total buy-in and keeping score on the credit meter affords you several advantages. If your strategy is to quit when you're ahead, your built-in scorekeeper lets you know when you've arrived.

If your strategy is to earn a profit, then try to hit the big jackpot, but not dip back into your original stake, you can monitor your progress by watching the meter.

If you have a loss limit, pre-loading these amounts into the machines helps reinforce the discipline you need to stay the course.

Some machines have bill acceptors attached to the side of the device (as in this photograph), while others are embedded in its face.

CHAPTER 2

ODDS & ODDS MAKING

ODDS-ON FAVORITES

The odds favor the casino in every case. But with some knowledge you can mitigate this house advantage. By understanding the casino edge and philosophy, players can have a good chance to win.

Take a look at Las Vegas today. Las Vegas Boulevard, the famous "Strip", has added new hotels at a rate of two per year in the Nineties. Excalibur, MGM Grand, Treasure Island and Luxor will soon be joined by New York-New York, Paris, Monte Carlo, Bellagio, and others. Atlantic City's 12 casinos are jammed for every hour of the 24 hours they're open, and several more are now on the drawing board. Even in sleepy Biloxi, Mississippi, casino action is non-stop, with more "dockside" casinos being added year after year.

What should all this expansion tell you? No, there isn't the need for new hotel rooms in Las Vegas. No, the beaches in Atlantic City aren't the most beautiful in the world. And no, people don't frequent the dockside casinos in Biloxi because they yearn for riverboat gambling of days past. This should tell you that the casinos make so much money that American casino companies are falling all over themselves—and spending hundreds of millions of dollars—to build the next one. And why are they making so much money? Because the games they offer in the casino don't offer the players much chance of winning. The tables have a built in house edge, and the slots are simply computers programmed to win more for the casino than they pay out.

Mathematics plays the most important role in the casino. The mathematicians who developed the rules of the various games that give the house its guaranteed wins are some of the casinos' most valued consultants.

Slot machines are easy. Slots are essentially computers that can be programmed to pay back a certain amount of the money deposited in them. A little device known as the "random number generator", an essential element in many different kinds of computers, determines when jackpots are hit, how many are hit, and for how much. No one can tell when it will happen, but casino executives are certain of one thing: when the day is over, a pre-determined amount of dollars will be added to the bottom line, courtesy of the slots.

Sure, you can win at slot machines. They all hit jackpots, and if you're lucky enough to be playing the machine when the jackpot hits, you could be a winner. But if you continue to play *ad infinitum*, you will lose. It's the law of averages, and it's a law that has no loopholes.

Video poker is different. If you know what machines to look for and how to play those machines when you find them, you can reduce the house advantage to as little as two percent or even less. But to beat that house advantage, you have to get your share of the jackpots—royal flushes, fives-of-a-kind, or whatever the top award might be. And that factor is dependent upon our old friend, the random number generator. Video poker gives you some control over the results by making your decisions matter. A skillful player will have a better idea of which cards to discard and so on.

That's where we draw the line in the casino. You have the best chance to win when you play games in which you have some control over the outcome. That narrows your choices considerably, and we'll discuss how each game is designed to determine where your decisions matter.

GAMES YOU CAN WIN

The house advantage is built in to all the casino games, but in some games, the decisions you make can reduce the house edge to its minimum, and you can give yourself more than an even chance of winning.

BLACKJACK

Blackjack is the only game where the player can actually attain an edge over the casino, but that is reserved for skilled card counters. A set of strategies have been devised by a series of blackjack experts beginning in the 1950s, but the strategies are difficult to master and only give the player a slight edge under ideal conditions, so it is difficult for even

	GAME	HIGHEST CASINO EDGE	LOWEST CASINO EDGE
SKILL GAMES	Poker	10% of pot	5% of pot
	Sports Betting	10% of winning bet	5% of winning bet
	Blackjack	20% or more	2% edge to player (card counting)
CASINO GAMES	Craps	16.66% (any seven)	1.41% and lower (pass line w/odds)
	Roulette	7.89% (five number bet)	1.35% (french "0" roulette w/ "en prison")
	Baccarat	14.1% (tie)	1.17% (bank)
	Slots	20% and more	3% or less
	Video Poker	20% and more	4-5% (full-pay machines w/expert strategy)
	Keno	25%	25%
	Big Six Wheel	22.2%	11.1%

Casino games can take as much or as little as the house desires. Competition keeps the odds lowest.

good blackjack players to utilize them. And casinos are constantly making adjustments to their rules to combat these strategies.

Unskilled blackjack players face a house advantage between five and ten percent. There is no set house advantage, because different rules affect the overall house edge—the number of decks, the dealing style and the betting restrictions all add to the house edge.

There is a way, without counting cards, to cut the house edge to its absolute minimum. By applying "basic strategy", a manner of playing that takes advantage of the rules which relate to the dealer's cards, you can reduce the house edge. Again, how much you can reduce the house edge depends on the rule variations, but basic strategy gives blackjack players their best chance to win.

POKER

The house has no advantage in poker, so to make its money, the casino traditionally takes a "rake"—a percentage of total wagers. In some casinos or at higher limit games, the house charges an hourly "seat rental" to stage the game. The rake or seat rental varies in most poker rooms, but because poker is a game of skill, your decisions are all-important.

In poker, your opponents are the other players, not the casino, so if you're skilled at poker, you should have the opportunity to win at least your share of the pots.

Unfortunately, poker is the most intimidating of all casino

games. This is because the other players depend upon you misplaying hands, so they'll use everything at their disposal, including intimidation, to force you to make mistakes. But there are few things more exhilarating in a casino than winning a big poker pot.

There are many different types of poker games, but we're going to concentrate on the two most popular games, seven-card stud and hold 'em.

SPORTS BETTING

Even though you'll only find legal sports betting in Nevada, it is clearly America's favorite wagering option. According to a 1990 article in the "Wall Street Journal", more than $25 billion is bet annually on sports in the US. Only $1.3 billion of that was bet legally in Nevada, but if you want to bet on sporting events without worrying about whether you will be paid, Nevada is the only place to be.

The reason you can win betting on sports is that, unlike most casino games like blackjack or craps, sport events are rarely played under ideal conditions. Weather, injuries, and freak plays all affect the outcome of games. But the most important reason you can profit from sports is that the oddsmakers set the lines based on how they believe the public will bet on the sporting event, not on which team or player should prevail.

The object of a sports book operation is to make the maximum amount of money without taking unreasonable risks. For example, in Nevada, you lay $11 to win $10. That odd dollar is called the "vig" or vigorish. Bookmakers in Nevada will try to balance the amount of money bet on each side of any sporting event so that they will not have to pay off more than they took in. The vig is their cushion.

GAMES YOU CAN'T WIN, BUT MIGHT LIKE TO TRY

Some games have a hefty house advantage and the results will almost always end up favoring the casino—no surprise there! But by intelligent, disciplined use of betting strategies, and your bankroll, you at least have the possibility of winning.

CRAPS
Statistically, the second-best bet in the casino is found on the craps table. The bettor is only backing a 1.4 percent disadvantage when playing the pass or don't pass lines. And when you add the "odds" bet, the casino edge can be reduced to less than 0.2 percent.

To get such advantages, however, you must risk a good deal of money. If your bankroll can't survive a loss when your big bet is on the table, craps can be a dangerous game.

BACCARAT

The casino's most glamorous game, the bank bet on the baccarat table is the casino's most advantageous bet. With a house edge of only 1.17 percent, baccarat offers one of the best chances to win.

But because baccarat is surrounded by ritual, and frequently hosts high rollers to the exclusion of average players, many people looking for the best bets often look elsewhere.

The complicated rules have no bearing on the way you play the game. The game is deceptively simple, and once you get used to the pampering you get in the baccarat pit, you may never return to the "masses" of blackjack or craps players.

ROULETTE

One of the world's most popular games, the American version of roulette is one of the worst bets in the casino. In a double "00" roulette game—the American version—you face a rather formidable 5.26 percent. In Atlantic City, a special rule reduces the odds on even money bets to 2.7 percent. French, or European roulette—the single "0" wheel—has that same 2.7 percent house edge for all bets. Roulette is an enjoyable game, but there are few opportunities to use either strategy or money management to combat those casino disadvantages.

GAMES YOU CAN'T WIN, PERIOD

There are some games in the casino that should be avoided at all costs. Barring a lucky streak akin to being struck by lightning, these games are weighted so much in the casino's favor it is foolish to even consider playing them. Try to avoid the temptation at all costs.

THE CASINO'S BEST AND WORST BETS

GAME	BET	HOUSE EDGE
Baccarat	Banker	1.17%
Baccarat	Player	1.63%
Craps	Pass Line	1.46%
Craps	Pass Line with double odds	0.61%
Craps	Pass Line with 5x odds	0.32%
Craps	Pass Line with 10x odds	0.18%
Roulette	Single "0"	2.7%
Roulette	Double "00"	5.6%
Blackjack	Single Deck*	0.0%
Blackjack	Double Decks*	0.35%
Blackjack	Four Decks*	0.52%
Blackjack	Eight Decks*	0.61%
Big Six Wheel	$5 Spot	11.1%
Keno	One Spot, 2-1 payoff	25.0%
Big Six Wheel	Joker	14.8%
Sic Bo	Small or Big	2.8%
Sic Bo	Two of a Kind	37.5%

LINKED PROGRESSIVE SLOT MACHINES

The "life-changing" prizes of the million-dollar-plus jackpots carry even greater odds than being struck by lightning. These machines are joined with others in many other casinos, giving you the chance to compete against billions of other combinations conjured up by the random number generator. Unless you believe a higher force is looking to provide you with a trouble-free life—and there must be plenty of people who do, judging from the receipts from state lotteries—avoid the multi-casino linked progressive slot machines. Unless you win the big prize, you're just making a donation because the chance you will even break even is almost nil.

In-house progressive slot machines with payouts in the hundreds of thousands are a little better, but not much.

BIG SIX WHEEL AND SIC BO

With a casino advantage between 11 percent and 22 percent, the Big Six Wheel, money wheel or wheel of fortune ranks as one of the worst bets in the house. Sure, you've seen the game on the boardwalks of seaside resorts and midways of your local carnivals, but the casino version isn't any better. And you can't even win a fluffy stuffed animal.

Sic Bo is the Oriental version of the Big Six Wheel. Instead of a wheel, however, it uses dice in a cage. On most bets, the house advantage ranges between 8 and 48 percent. The only

saving grace is the "big" and "small" bets which offer a much more reasonable 2.8 percent house edge. If you play, don't be tempted to play any other bets.

KENO

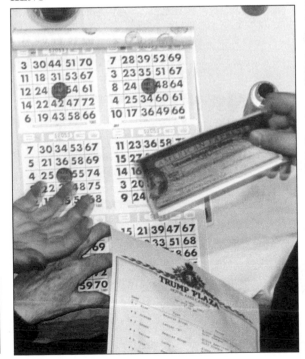

This relative to bingo is actually more like a lottery. From a pool of 80 numbers, you can pick anywhere between one and 20 numbers. The odds are determined by each house, but the house edge is generally greater than 20 percent.

The one good thing about keno is that it offers you the least amount of losses per hour if you're betting $2 for each game. Since there are rarely more than six games an hour, you can relax in the keno lounge and keep guzzling those free drinks, without worrying that you're going to mess up your keno strategy. In fact, there is no valid keno strategy!

That said, anyone can be a winner at any casino game over the short term. The deviations from the long-term advantage for the casino can sometimes swing wildly. Everyone has heard of players who have been "struck by lightning" and win the multi-million dollar progressive jackpots, or those who win the lottery.

There are inveterate keno players who swear that they can overcome the hefty disadvantage they face when playing their favorite game.

And roulette, craps, baccarat, blackjack, and every other casino game has the same stories of gamblers struck by "dumb luck". Sure, it's all possible, but to make it anywhere close to probable, you've got to play the games that give you the most chances to win and you've got to use all your resources to give yourself an edge.

MONEY MANAGEMENT

One of the most talked about—and misunderstood— concepts in gambling is money management. Countless articles and books have been written about the subject, but

PROGRESSIVE BETTING SYSTEM

$5 bet + Win = $10 bet	*$10 bet + Win = $20 bet*
$10 bet + Win = $15 bet	*$20 bet + Win = $30 bet*
$15 bet + Win = $20 bet	*$30 bet + Win = $40 bet*
$20 bet + Win = $10 bet	*$40 bet + Win = $20 bet*
Profit = $30	*Profit = $60*
$5 bet + Loss = $5 bet	

because of its slippery nature, few people really understand its implications.

Even the definitions of money management vary from expert to supposed expert. Some express disdain about a concept that can't be quantified by mathematical equations, and can only be described as an instinct. Others embrace it as the only real way to come out a winner in the end.

Money management in gambling is not like money management in real life, because in real life there is a source of guaranteed income via jobs or other payments. In a casino, the only guarantee is that the casino will win in the long run, so managing your money as you would in real life makes little sense.

WINNING MORE, LOSING LESS

The essential goal behind money management is to bet more when you're winning, and less when you're losing. This is, of course, easier said than done, and virtually impossible to attain. If you knew when you were going to win or lose, it wouldn't be called gambling.

The idea that managing your money can result in more winning sessions than losing sessions is difficult to swallow since all casino games have negative expectations for the player. That is, the casino has the edge at all times, and money management will do nothing to reduce or even ameliorate that advantage.

What money management will accomplish, however, is to extend your playing time, enabling you to remain in action when the inevitable winning streak finally arrives.

Most of the reasoning behind this belief is that you will set a bet progression that will take advantage of winning streaks and minimize losses.

Let's look at a typical betting progression that could accomplish this goal. You should always think in term of "units", which are the basic bets that allow you to track your play more easily. Playing the minimum bet at blackjack, you'd bet one unit, say $5. After a win, you'd bet $10, or two units. If you win the $10 bet, take back one unit, and bet $15. After a third win, you would take back two units, and make a $20 bet. In the unlikely circumstance that you'd win four in a row, you take back all the units, and start again, but this time with two units ($10). This way, you maximize your profits, while minimizing your exposure to the sure loss. If at any point you lose during this progression, return to the original one unit bet.

There are as many betting systems as there are players, but only by sticking with a predetermined system will you have the opportunity to walk away a winner.

One betting system that runs contrary to any "money management" system is trying to replenish your bankroll after losing by making progressively larger bets. This is called "chasing your money", and is a shortcut to the infamous "gambler's ruin", which is an aphorism for going broke.

BETTING BANKROLL

Another area of dispute among gambling experts is what comprises a comfortable bankroll and, of course, how best you can utilize it.

How big is big enough when you set out to play any game? To play any casino game effectively, a player must be comfortable with his betting level, and that's where the concept of "scared money" comes from. If you don't believe that you can compete effectively at a particular game with the money you have allocated, you should be playing another game or a lower minimum game. If you can't afford to play the money you are gambling, you shouldn't be playing. And if you believe you can recoup your loses by tapping the cash machine one more time, cut up your credit card. You definitely shouldn't be playing.

At blackjack, many experts suggest that a $5 player should have at least $250, but $100 can be enough if you carefully limit your time at the table. At a $5 craps game, a player should have at least 100 times the minimum bet because of the side bets that must be taken in order to take advantage of all the betting options craps has to offer. Other games don't have such stringent requirements and depend upon how you play the games, but players would be well advised to be able to absorb at least a loss of 20 units in roulette, baccarat, and slots.

BANKROLL STRATEGIES

Just like real life, money management has more to do with how you budget your bankroll, rather than simply the size of your bets. Most gambling experts suggest that you determine how long you plan to play in the casino, and set win goals and loss limits. Write them down and keep to them. You should therefore divide your bankroll into separate sessions accordingly.

For instance, if you're traveling to a casino destination for a two-day stay with a $2,000 bankroll, divide that stash into two $1,000 sessions. Then take each $1,000, and slice into four $250 sessions that will be designated for two-hour periods. Find that lucky slot machine or table, and get yourself started.

Play with discipline and knowledge, and if you win 50 percent of your session, $125 in this case, quit playing. Never stop in the middle of a streak, but as soon as it's obviously over, step away. Take that $375 and put it away. Some players actually bring envelopes with them. When they reach their win goal, they slide the cash in the envelope and mail it home.

If you can't afford a $2,000 bankroll, use a similar formula for the money you can afford.

Remember, when you win, you are not playing with the "casino's money". The only money the casino has is sitting in the dealer's chip rack. When it arrives on your side of the table it's your money, not the casino's. If you refer to it as the casino's money, there's a good chance it will be in a very short time.

If you lose the $250, take a walk. There's no point in setting loss limits unless you've the discipline to stick to them. Sit in the lounge. Check out the sports book. Or even go to your room and read this book. Whatever you do, it's got to be better than losing. Resist the desire to grab the next session bankroll. You can wait for luck to find you. She's never where you look, especially after she's been so elusive.

Time is your enemy. Remember, the longer you gamble, the more exposure you give to the casino's inescapable mathematical advantage.

THAT WINNING FEELING

The only way to win is to walk away a winner. Sure, it sounds simplistic, but think about it. How many times have you been up a decent amount of money in a casino, only to lose it all back and then some? It may have happened just minutes after you begin to play, so you can't stop then, can you? Of course you can! Discipline is the answer, and without it, you're doomed to lose.

In many ways, money management is knowing when to quit. And it's always better to quit on your own terms, rather than the casino's.

When to quit is often a function of why you gamble to begin with. Do you see gambling as simply an enjoyable pastime that will cost you a few bucks as a "price" for the entertainment it provides? Do you gamble for the adrenaline rush that you get when that maximum bet is out there? Or do you enjoy the competition that pits you against the dealer and the other players?

No one can tell you when to quit. Only you can determine whether that particular gambling session has fulfilled the desire that gambling sparks. But very few players enjoy losing, so the idea for virtually everyone, is to quit while you're ahead.

As you can see, money management is simply about survival. If you lose all your money within the first few hours after arriving in a casino, you're in for a long ride home or an even longer wait to catch that ride home. Not only can money management give you a better chance to become a winner, but even if you do lose your entire bankroll, you'll have the satisfaction of knowing that you've given yourself the best chance to win.

GETTING THE BEST OF THE TABLES

Casinos spend millions of dollars in promoting their games. Everyone knows about how casinos bring in high rollers,

treat them to a room, food, beverage and entertainment in exchange for a chance to dent their bankroll.

The casinos are betting that the money they advance to host the high roller is an investment that will be returned when the player hits the tables, or, today, even the slots. To qualify for such a "complimentary" or comp, a player has to demonstrate that he is indeed a high roller by giving casino executives the action they expect.

The level of betting to qualify as a "high roller" varies from casino to casino. At a small casino in northern Nevada, a high roller might be someone who bets $25 a hand at blackjack. At one of the glamorous Las Vegas Strip casino resorts, it might take a $500 a hand average bet to even attract attention.

The point is that a casino is willing to return a certain percentage of your action in complimentaries, whether you are playing slots or table games. You don't have to be a high roller; you don't even have to be a regular customer. Most important, you don't even have to lose; all you have to do is satisfy their qualifications for time played and average bet.

TABLE TALK

The key to being recognized as a regular player, and to therefore receive the benefits that are distributed to regular players, is to get rated.

Getting rated is simple. In most casinos, you can use the same card issued by the slot clubs to be rated at either the slots or the table games. So before you begin to play, stop by the slot promotions booth and sign up. They will ask your name, address, 'phone number, and most likely specialized information, such as your game preferences, birthday, anniversary and other information that will enable them to tailor special promotions to specific audiences.

To be rated at the tables means that the supervisors, or "floorpersons", track your betting style, from the amount of money you buy in for, and the time you spend playing, to your average bet. They even note how well you play the game, for that will be evaluated, as well, when they determine the comps you are eligible for.

Getting rated at the tables also gives you the opportunity to speak with the casino personnel, from the dealers and the floorpersons to the pit boss, who oversees the action in his "pit", or collection of tables. They will be most helpful in clearing up any questions about how to play the game, the payouts and the procedures for obtaining comps. If you're not satisfied with the answers or the attitudes of the personnel assigned to that table, move on. There are plenty of options, particularly if you're playing in Atlantic City or Las Vegas.

SLOT CLUBS

In the past, casinos rated only those customers who played table games. The customers' play was observed by casino floor personnel who calculated the average dollar amount the customer played per hour. Players who exclusively frequented slot machines could rarely attain the "high roller" category and receive the same complimentaries and extra services given to those rated as high-action players.
In recent years, however, the rating of slot players has become common throughout the casino industry. This change was made necessary by the increase in the casinos' slot revenues and made possible by modern technology. With slot revenue accounting for the large majority of gross gaming revenues, it became important to find a way to track these players in order to encourage them to return to play again and again.

The casinos' ability to track the activity of slot players was provided by electronic systems developed by most of the major slot manufacturers. Under these systems, players who apply are issued cards similar to credit cards to be inserted into specially designed slot machines. Each slot machine and video poker machine is connected to a central computer which contains information on customers' playing histories.

When the system has identified the player by their card, it flashes them a greeting on an electronic display ("Hi Bob") and tells them how many bonus points they have accumulated so far and how many coins they must play to get another point. As they drop in coins, the display counts down the number of coins remaining to be played until they get their next point. At one Las Vegas casino, for example, a player must drop 20 one-dollar coins, 40 half-dollars or 80 quarters, to earn a bonus point.

Slot clubs serve a dual purpose for the casinos. They are designed to attract players by offering a bonus. Players can earn points toward comps, special merchandise or even "cashback", which is essentially a cash award for patronizing a particular casino. But the systems function primarily as player tracking devices. The data fed into the central computer from each card allows the casino to determine who the "high rollers" are, the amount and frequency of play, which machines are most popular, how often and for what reason machines malfunction, total revenue per machine, frequency of jackpots, percentage of profits for the casino, and other accounting data that is valuable to casinos.

It simply makes sense to sign up for the slot club in any casino where you might play the slots. While you may not play to the level that would qualify you for comps or cashback, you may be included in a valuable promotional campaign. Casinos are always looking to add loyal customers, and often go through their databases and "prospect" for players by offering free tokens, meals, entertainment or hotel rooms. You want your name on the list when these goodies are passed out.

HERE COME THE COMPS

Comps come in all shapes and sizes. If you spend any amount of time in a casino playing a reasonable amount of money, you should be eligible for comps.

The formula that qualifies players for comps varies from casino to casino. Some casinos are more generous with their comps because they believe that the level of play they receive from the players in return more than justifies the expense, while other casinos don't see the reason to "give away the store" when players will give them a good share of play whether they get comped or not.

How do you know whether you've met their guidelines in getting comped? The only way to truly know is to ask! It's

that simple. If you're playing the tables, call the supervisor over, and explain you'd like to get a break and get something to eat. If you haven't played long enough, or bet enough, he'll tell you. If you have, he'll suggest a meal in a coffee shop or other low-line restaurant.

After a while, you'll get a feel about how much you play, and how much you deserve. Don't argue, however. Casino personnel are accountable for the comps they issue, so it's difficult to get them to upgrade your comp if you really don't deserve it. If you feel you're being "lowballed," ask to see the pit boss. They are the ones ultimately responsible, so he or she will be pleased to explain their comp policies in greater detail. The buck truly stops here.

CREDIT
WHERE IT IS DUE

Most people carry cash to the casino. Since cash is the fuel of the gaming business, it is the essential tool of the games. But carrying cash can be dangerous, particularly when you're on holiday.

There are other options to bringing a pocketful of cash with you to the casino.

Travelers checks are a good choice. As they are with any other business, travelers checks are as good as cash in the casino. They offer security and peace of mind to the player, but sometimes are difficult to handle. Exchanging travelers checks is easy enough. Simply take them to the casino cage and you will receive cash. Losing travelers checks means you must track down a representative of the company that issued them, but that is generally not very hard in a casino jurisdiction where most companies maintain offices.

Another option is to bring your ATM card to the casino destination. If you subscribe to a system that is widespread,

you'll usually be able find a machine, but eventually, you still have to walk around with cash, albeit not as much as you would normally bring at one time.

Cash advances from your credit card are very convenient, but not recommended. Most casinos have cash advance machines right on their casino floor. These are a very profitable business for their owners, as well as for the casinos where they are located.

Players in the heat of the moment in need of some cash are usually the victims of these advances. The charge on a cash advance is prohibitive, especially when combined with the usurious rates normally charged for credit card balances. The best advice is to leave your credit cards in your hotel room before entering the casino.

Most serious gamblers and frequent casino guests have established credit with the casino. Casino credit enables them to travel with the minimum amount of cash, and to deal with a casino on the same level as a bank. You make withdrawals and deposits.

Yes, casino credit can be dangerous. Like everything involved with gambling, casino credit requires discipline. But if you plan to frequent a casino destination on a regular basis and want to travel without the fear of losing your cash, it makes the most sense of any of the "cashless" options.

Establishing credit is easy. Simply head to the casino cashier and explain that you would like to establish credit. They will point you to a credit executive or a casino host. You fill out a form very similar to one you'd use to apply for a credit card. You're asked for bank account numbers, the status of your home ownership, and several credit references—credit cards, auto loans and so on.

Most US casinos use the same credit reporting agency. It is identical to most of the companies that gather credit information for traditional business transactions. It will examine your finances and then recommend whether to accept or reject your application. If you're accepted, you will be given a credit limit, similar to the limit issued for a traditional credit card. This is called your "line".

Once you're approved, you can draw on that line at any gaming table or slot machine. When you approach a gaming table you tell the dealer you'd like a "marker". A marker is simply a counter check like you'd find in a bank. You then give the supervisor your name and the amount you'd like to withdraw. He will put it in the system, and within five minutes, the marker will be ready. You sign it, and the dealer counts out chips in the amount of your marker.

Besides not having to carry a large amount of cash, the advantage of using casino credit is that you have a clear record of your gaming bankroll. That doesn't help much if you lose it all, but if you employ the money management techniques described in this chapter, casino credit can be valuable tool. You are also automatically rated when you take a marker, so you never have to worry if a supervisor is watching your action.

The casino wants to encourage you to use casino credit, so in most cases, they don't charge interest on the money they loan you for at least 30 days. If you are disciplined with the use of casino credit and you pay off the balance quickly upon returning home, casino credit can be a bonus for the knowledgeable player.

THE SYSTEMS APPROACH

HOW TO WIN EVEN WHEN YOU'RE LOSING

It almost seems as if the car knows its way, carrying Ross and Marie Winslow down the Garden State Parkway, as it slashes through the South Jersey pinelands. The Winslows make the ride from Morris Plains to Atlantic City about three times a month to enjoy a little entertainment, food and gambling. The real reason, however, is that Ross thinks he's got the casinos' number. "They pay me to gamble with them, but I'm going to make the trip anyway," he says. "I just have a ball there."

Ross and Marie are $1 slot players; Ross prefers video poker, while Marie is still trying to hit the big progressive jackpot that will allow them to retire a few years early.

As slot players become consistently more important to the casinos, the Winslows are wooed by Atlantic City hotels with increasing ardor. "At first, you'd just get two for the buffet, or maybe a reduced rate on a room," says Ross, "but now, you can get free food, free rooms or cash back."

Ross has it down to a science. He spreads out his play between three or four properties and has become an expert on the minimum play for the maximum benefits. He knows, for instance, that it's not how much you win or lose, but how much you play. "I don't understand why people play only one coin at a time," he says. "It takes them twice as long get a good rating, and they miss out on the big jackpot, if it hits."

While the Winslows don't fool themselves that the casinos are giving out something for nothing, they like the attention and the perks that come with being "loyal" customers. "The slot hosts at other casinos know I play in other houses, too," Ross says. "They don't care, as long as I give them their fair share."

Marie says they didn't worry about getting rated until one casino began offering cash rebates for a certain amount of play. "I never wanted that merchandise they gave out with a lot of play," she says. "Give me the cash, and I'll buy what I want."

Now, both Ross and Marie carry an accordion billfold to hold their numerous slot-club cards. Marie has two of each. "If I'm playing two machines," she explains, "I want to be able to get rated on each machine."

What is it that makes the casinos give cash to its customers, when it is actually trying to get as much of their cash as possible? "If we give them good service, and they enjoy playing in our casino," says one casino slot vice president, "they'll give us that cash back and more."

Ross understands that attitude but claims he makes every trip with his eyes open. "I know they can't build these places without some suckers," he admits. "I think we're fair to each other, though. I give them a shot at my money, and they give me whatever they think they can afford; it's a two-way street."

CHAPTER 3

BLACKJACK

FEELING LIKE 21

Blackjack, the most popular casino game, offers the best chance at winning. Players with varying levels of expertise in card counting can gain an edge over the house, and even casual players can play close to even.

There was a time when craps was the most popular casino game in America. Two world wars and a "police action" developed craps players who crowded the tables of Reno and Las Vegas, as well as the many illegal casinos across the country in the middle part of this century.

In the mid-Fifties, a group of mathematicians discovered that a "basic strategy" could be employed to reduce the house edge at blackjack, or "21", to virtually nothing. Casinos suddenly realized that the game could be beaten, and have predictably taken various precautions to protect it ever since.

The publication of "Beat the Dealer" by Ed Thorp in 1962 began a rush to discover systems and methods that would indeed beat the dealer. Card counting, the method first described by Thorp, has been refined over the years, and today, casinos employ various methods from shuffling after every hand to actually barring players accused of card counting from playing in casinos.

The casinos like to call blackjack a game of chance, but it is as much a game of skill as anything. But you won't hear the casinos denying very strongly that blackjack can be beaten. After all, casinos make most of the money they make at the table games via blackjack. It's great advertising when someone reports a big win at the blackjack tables. Players have been encouraged for many years to believe that blackjack can be beaten, and the casinos don't want to do anything to disrupt that message.

But becoming an effective card counter is difficult and time consuming. And unless you're planning to make blackjack your occupation, it's unnecessary.

Blackjack can be played successfully by using variations on the "basic strategy" developed by that group of mathematicians in the Fifties. But first, let's review how the game operates in a casino.

PLAYING THE GAME

Blackjack's popularity grew as much at the kitchen table as at the casino table. It was an easy game to learn and to deal. But you have to realize that the game played at the kitchen table is very different from the one found in casinos around the world.

30

Even if you've played the game in a casino after having learned it at home, it's important to review the basics of the game. While you might know when to hit or stand, the key to winning at blackjack is knowing when to split and double down.

THE BIG DEAL

The blackjack table in a casino is generally set up with seven betting spots, although some games have as few as five. A permanent dealer acts for the house and stands behind the table to distribute the cards.

When you've decided upon the game you want to play by examining the sign that announces the minimum and maximum wagers, you will buy in for chips, as we discussed in Chapter One. Do not place your money in the betting circle, however. Some casinos permit cash to play on the first bet, and you may lose your entire stake on one hand. Instead, set it to one side and wait for the dealer to convert it into chips.

After you receive your chips, start small. Place the minimum bet in the circle in front of your seat.

Casino blackjack differs from the kitchen table variety in many ways. At home, you probably only used one deck, as do a few casinos in Downtown Las Vegas and Reno. However, most casinos use multiple decks ranging from two up to eight.

The blackjack dealer shuffles the cards, and if he's dealing more than two decks, he'll place the shuffled cards in a box known as a "shoe". After he shuffles, he'll ask a player to "cut" the deck, by using a yellow card, known as the cut card. The

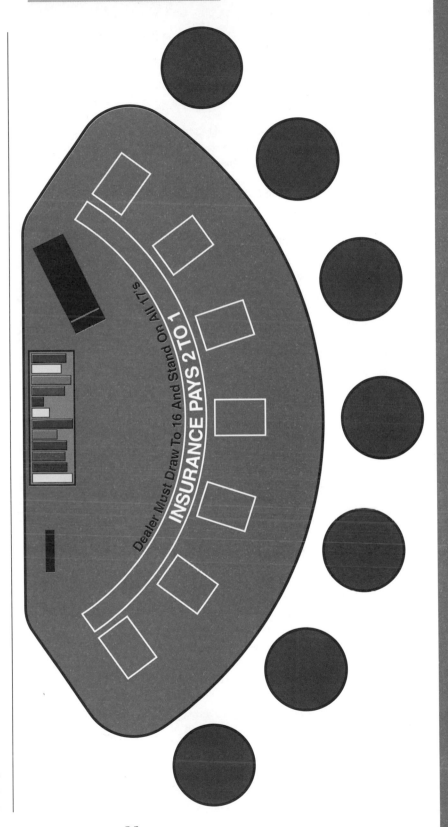

player simply slides the yellow card into the deck at any point. The dealer divides the deck at the cut point, and takes the cut card and places it about two-thirds the way into the deck. This deck "penetration" varies from casino to casino, and sometimes even from table to table.

The dealer then places the cards into the shoe, or arranges them in his hand (for two or less decks). The dealer will then discard—"burn"—the first card, and check to make sure that all players have their bets in the right place and in the right amount. He begins distributing the cards to the players from the front of the shoe or the top of the deck.

He'll begin with the player farthest to his left—known as "first base"—and then proceed to give one card to each player, including the dealer's "upcard." He'll repeat the motion until every player has two cards. He completes the deal by sliding his "hole card" under his upcard.

In some casinos in Nevada, the players are allowed to handle the cards. In this situation, the players receive their cards face down, and pick them up with their hands. If you're playing this type of game, do not use two hands to pick the cards up. Pick them up with one hand and hold them over the table. Never remove them from the table or shield them in any manner from the dealer's view. The dealer is responsible for the security of the cards, and must prevent them from being replaced by other cards or tampered with in any way.

In other casinos in most other jurisdictions, the players' cards are dealt face up, and the players are prohibited from touching them at all. The dealer has to handle all the cards and chips.

PLAYING YOUR HAND

It doesn't matter how many players are seated at the table. Blackjack is essentially a one-on-one showdown between yourself and the dealer. The players are not trying to beat each other, only the dealer. Each player is playing a separate game. The only thing the players have in common is that their cards come from the same deck and are distributed by the same dealer.

The object of blackjack is to beat the dealer. The winner is whoever has closest to a total of 21. You reach 21 by adding up the values of the cards. Tens and face cards are worth ten points, the other cards count as their numerical values, and Aces are worth one or 11, at the discretion of the player.

For example, an Eight of clubs and a Seven of hearts is 15. A King of spades and a Queen of diamonds counts as 20. An Ace of hearts and a Five of hearts can count as 16 or six.

You determine the valuation of the Ace, and can decide to change it in mid-hand. In the last example, for instance, say you draw an Eight to the Ace and Five. That would "bust" your hand if the Ace was counted as 11, so you drop it to a one. In that situation, you count it as one, and you've got 14.

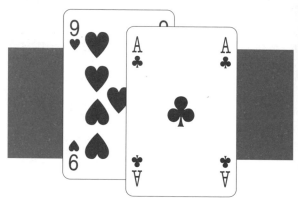

A "soft hand" is a hand that contains an Ace.

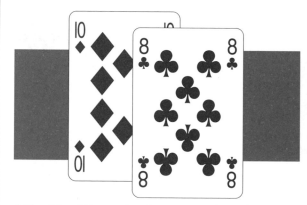

A "hard hand" is one that does not contain an Ace.

After the dealer gives each player two cards, he'll return to first-base and start acting on each hand individually. He will point to your cards when it is your turn. If you want another card—a "hit"—you indicate by scratching the table with your hand. The dealer will not accept a verbal command because the hand signal must be given so that the security cameras can see exactly what you want to do with that hand. If you want to "stand"—take no cards—you indicate by waving your hand, palm down. You use that motion when you've decided to stop taking additional cards, as well.

In the hand-held game, you scrape the table with the edge of your cards to indicate you want to hit. When you're satisfied with your hand, you slide your cards under your chips in the betting circle.

If you take a hit and that card puts your total over 21, you lose automatically. The dealer removes your cards and your chips. In the hand-held game, turn your cards over immediately if you've exceeded 21, so the dealer can finish your hand.

At the end of the hand, if your cards total closer to 21, you win! If the dealer's hand is closer to 21, you lose. And if you tie the dealer—called a "push"—no one wins or loses.

After the dealer acts on the hands of all the players—giving each the opportunity to hit or stand—he begins to settle the bets. If the dealer has busted, he pays all the hands that remain. If you busted during the course of the game, you're out of luck. Only those hands that are "live" get paid.

If the dealer hasn't busted, he will pay the winners and take the losers' chips. If you have pushed, the dealer will rap the table with his knuckles and leave the chips where they stand. You are then allowed to increase, decrease or remove the bet.

BJ!
There is one way to win automatically at blackjack, and that is to receive a total of 21 in the first two cards. That requires a ten-value card and an Ace. This is called a "natural" or a "blackjack".

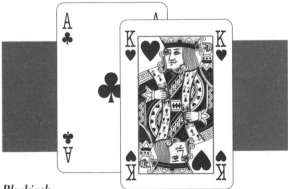

Blackjack

When a player receives a blackjack, he wins a bonus. Normally, all bets are paid off at even money when playing blackjack, but when you get a blackjack, you receive a

three-to-two payoff. If you've bet $10, you'll get paid $15, for example.

If you're playing the hand-held game, you should turn your cards over immediately to get paid.

The only time a player can receive a blackjack and not get paid immediately is if the dealer also has a blackjack. In this case, it's a push, and no one gets paid. You can protect yourself by taking "insurance", an option we'll discuss later in this chapter.

DOUBLING DOWN
One of the attractions of blackjack is the ability to increase your bets in mid-hand if you feel you have a good opportunity to win. This is the main reason that blackjack can be played nearly even. When you have the chance to make these bets, you should take advantage of them.

One of the circumstances in which you may increase your bet is called doubling down. This means the casino will allow you to make a second bet equal in size to your first bet. In return for this right, you agree to accept only one more card for your hand. You can double down only after looking at your first two cards. You cannot take a hit and double down. Some casinos allow you to double down for less than the amount of your original bet. This should be avoided because if the situation is worth doubling down, it is worth betting as much as you can, which is the amount of your original bet.

To tell the dealer you want to double down, you slide a second wager next to your original wager in the betting circle. Do not place the additional bet on top of the original wager, because the dealer may think you are trying to cheat by increasing your bet illegally.

No hand signal is necessary. The dealer will see your double-down bet and give you one card, generally placed horizontally across the first two cards. In the hand-held game, the dealer will place the card under your chips in the betting circle. You may pick up the card to see what you've been given, but you'll get more respect if you wait until the dealer settles all bets to expose your hand.

If you win your bet, you'll be paid even money for the two bets, and receive double your original wager. If you lose, of course, both bets are taken away. In the event of a push, you keep both bets, but are not paid.

SPLITTING

The second option to increase your original wager is known as "splitting". When you receive two cards of the same value, you are allowed to match your original bet, and split the two cards into separate hands. You are not required to split; you can play the hand like any other hand, but in some situations, it is advantageous to make two hands out of a pair. It is entirely up to you.

Each card of the pair becomes the first card of a separate, totally independent, hand, and each wager—the original bet and the second bet—applies only to the hand to which it is attached. The dealer gives one additional card on the first hand, and then takes instructions on additional hits. When that hand is completed, the second hand proceeds in the same manner.

Since the two hands are independent, you may win both, lose both or win one and lose one. To split a hand, place an identical bet next to your original bet. The wager must be the exact amount; it cannot be any more or any less.

Depending upon the rules of the individual casino, you may be able to split hands up to four times. For example, if you have two Eights, split them, and receive a third Eight, you may split that hand to make three independent hands. The rules concerning how many times you may split vary from casino to casino.

The only card that has different splitting rules is the Ace. When you receive two Aces and split them, you only receive one card on each Ace. If that card is a ten-value card, it is simply a count of 21, not a blackjack, which must appear in the first two original cards.

In many casinos, you may also double down after splitting. The same rules apply for doubling down on a split hand as would for an original hand.

PEEKING

In most casinos today, if the dealers have an Ace or a Ten-value card up, they play the hand through, and if they have blackjack, all double down, and split bets are returned to the players, who only lose their original bets. Since this wastes time and causes some player discontent, some casinos allow dealers to "peek" at their hole card to determine whether they have a blackjack. If they have blackjack, they immediately turn it over and take all losing bets, which saves time and aggravation.

Occasionally, you can find a dealer who "gives away" the value of his hole card (when he doesn't have a hold card that completes a blackjack). This is called a "dealer tell". You have to understand body language or psychology, but this has been one of the most consistent winning blackjack secrets down through the years.

Recently, technology has been employed to speed up the game. Several companies have marketed laser devices that will read the value of a card by slipping the edge of the card through a narrow opening. It tells the dealer whether that card is a Ten or an Ace, but not the specific value of the card. This allows him to complete the game without the knowledge of the value of the hole card, once again saving time, but also preventing dealer tells.

THE INSURANCE POLICY

At a blackjack table, there is perhaps no bigger argument than whether the player should insure a blackjack. When the dealer turns an Ace as the upcard, he will ask the players if they'd like to "insure" their hands. If the player accepts the bet, which must be taken before any action is taken on any players' hand, the player puts up one-half of his original bet, and if the insurance wager wins (meaning the dealer has blackjack), it pays off at two-to-one odds.

When the player is dealt, for instance, a Queen and an Ace, and the dealer has an Ace showing, there is a great propensity on the part of the player to "protect" that hand by buying insurance. After all, the logic goes, the blackjack is a bonus hand, which pays off at three-to-two odds. The dealer doesn't give out too many blackjacks, so players feel they had better get something out of that hand. If they have a blackjack and the dealer also has one, it's a push (a tie) and the player gets nothing.

By taking insurance, the player reasons he will always end up with a profit. That thinking is logical, but it's also flawed. In a 52-card deck, there are 16 Ten-value cards, and 36 non-Tens, a ratio of 2.25 to one. When you are faced with the situation in which we have a two-card blackjack and the dealer has an Ace showing, there are now 15 Tens and 34 non-Tens remaining, which gives you a ratio of 2.27 to one. Since insurance pays only two-to-one, you're getting the worst of it on that basis alone.

Let's say you've got a $10 bet and are dealt a blackjack while the dealer has an Ace showing. There are four different results that can occur:

● You take insurance and the dealer has blackjack;
● You take insurance and the dealer does not have blackjack;
● You do not take insurance and the dealer has blackjack;
● You do not take insurance and the dealer does not have blackjack.

In the first two results, the player wins $10. If the player bets $10 and insures for $5, he'll push the original bet and win $10 on the insurance bet. If the dealer doesn't have blackjack, the player wins $15 from the original bet, but loses the $5 insurance bet, leaving a $10 profit.

In the third result, you have not wagered on insurance, and tied the dealer with your blackjack. You keep your $10 bet, giving you a net gain of zero. In scenario four, you beat the dealer with your blackjack, giving you a gain of $15 on the hand. In three situations, you make money, while in the remaining one, you win nothing.

When you have a blackjack and the dealer shows an Ace, theoretically, there are 15 Tens and 34 non-Tens left in the deck, making a possible total of 49 cards remaining. Since the dealer has to have a Ten in the hole to complete a two-card blackjack, he has to get one of those Tens, which give him a possibility of 30.6 percent of having blackjack. That means that 69.4 percent of the time, the dealer will not have blackjack. Clearly, results two and four are going to happen much more often than results one and three.

Your most profitable result, therefore, is the one which also occurs the vast majority of the time. Without boring you with the math, you are gaining a very worthwhile 4.1 percent by not insuring.

The truth is, in no situation should anyone playing basic strategy execute the insurance option. The only player who would gain is someone using a card-counting strategy.

THE WHITE FLAG

Another option that is offered in some casinos is surrender. This only occurs when the dealer has an Ace or a Ten-value card up. If you do not like your first two cards, and believe you cannot beat the dealer, you may announce "surrender".

It is the only play you make verbally at the blackjack table and it can work to your advantage.

There are two types of surrender—early or late. In "late surrender", you announce your intention, but the dealer marks your bet, either with a "lammer"—a plastic chip—or he places your chips on top of your cards. If the dealer has blackjack, he takes your entire bet. If he does not have blackjack, you get half your bet back.

If you decide to surrender, and the dealer immediately takes half your bet, you have found a casino that offers "early surrender". This is the best type of surrender because you get half your bet back whether or not the dealer has blackjack.

BASIC STRATEGY

Understanding and perfecting basic strategy in blackjack can make the difference between winning and losing. Outside of poker, where the players compete against each other, not the house, blackjack is the only casino table game where the player can affect the outcome by his skillful play.

While card-counting may yield slightly greater results, basic strategy is much easier and can be mastered by learning a few key rules. Luck still plays a major role in the outcome of playing sessions, but over the long term, basic strategy gives a player the best chance of winning.

Playing situations vary widely at casinos in the United States. For maximum benefit, basic strategy should be altered for different conditions. Basic strategy players looking to get the best of the casino should look for situations where they have the best chance before they even sit down to play.

The single most important variable is the number of decks used. Players want games that use as few decks as possible. One deck is ideal, but two or four decks can also provide positive situations. Games dealt with six or eight decks are more difficult to beat. Keep in mind that the number of decks can vary not only from casino to casino, but also from table to table within the same casino.

Rules also vary between jurisdiction, and, ideally, basic strategy should also be altered to account for these differences. The most important rule variation is the dealer hitting or standing on soft 17. In Downtown Las Vegas, for instance, dealers hit a soft 17, which adds to the house advantage. On the Las Vegas Strip and in Atlantic City, dealers stand on all 17s.

Also important are restrictions on doubling down and splitting pairs. In some casinos, players are only permitted to double down on card totals of 10 and 11, another rule adding to the house edge. In some Caribbean islands, doubling down is only permitted on 11, further reducing a player's chance of winning. Other casinos restrict the number of times players can split pairs. Since players

theoretically only split pairs when they have the advantage to begin with, the casinos that deny additional splits want to limit their exposure. It is for that reason that many casinos also bar players from doubling down after splitting, another option that adds to the players' advantage.

Whenever possible, players should look for the most liberal rules when scouting out a positive blackjack situation. The following review of basic strategy is applicable for any playing situation, but players who want to obtain the best chance of winning must remember that different rules and conditions may affect the outcome.

HITTING AND STANDING

The most important decisions a player has to make is whether to hit or stand on particular hard and soft hands. Fortunately, the choices are rather straightforward. For hard hands, if the player's cards total 12 or higher, there are three simple rules:

● If the dealer shows a Seven or higher, hit if the player hand totals 12 through 16.

● Stand on any hand totaling 17 or above.

ALWAYS HIT, NEVER STAND

ALWAYS STAND, NEVER SPLIT

● Stand if the player cards total 12 through 16 and the dealer shows a Two through Six.

ALWAYS STAND

On soft hands, hit and stand as follows:
- If the dealer shows an Eight or less, players stand on soft 18 and more. Players always stand on soft 19 and above.

Player's cards   *Dealer's upcard*

ALWAYS STAND, NEVER DOUBLE

- Players always draw to soft 17 or less. Players only draw on soft 18 if the dealer shows an Eight, Nine or Ten.

Player's cards   *Dealer's upcard*

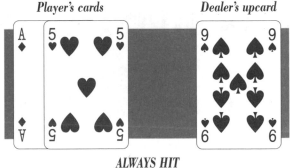

ALWAYS HIT

DOUBLING DOWN

The advantages of basic strategy kick in when the player has an opportunity to increase his bet, by doubling down or splitting. It is important to know the double-down situations in which the player has the advantage, because this is the chief method through which players reduce the house edge. Three basic rules govern this play for hard hands:

- Double down when the player's cards total 11 and the dealer shows a Ten or less.

Player's cards   *Dealer's upcard*

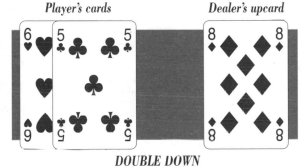

DOUBLE DOWN

- Double down when the player's cards total nine and the dealer shows a Four, Five or Six.

Player's cards   *Dealer's upcard*

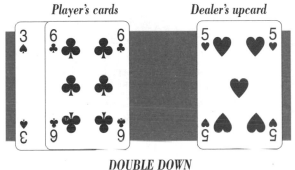

DOUBLE DOWN

- Double down when the player's cards total 10 and the dealer show a Nine or less.

Player's cards   *Dealer's upcard*

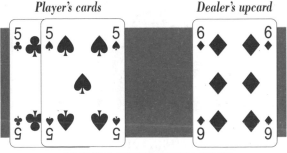

ALWAYS DOUBLE, NEVER SPLIT

For soft hands, three rules also are essential:
- Players double down with a soft 13 and soft 14 when the dealer shows a Five or Six.

Player's cards   *Dealer's upcard*

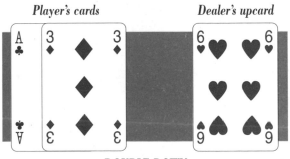

DOUBLE DOWN

● Players double down with a soft 15 and soft 16 when the dealer shows a Four, Five or Six.

Player's cards   *Dealer's upcard*

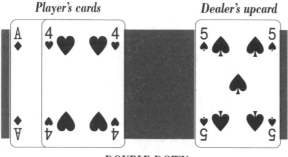

DOUBLE DOWN

● Players double down with a soft 17 and soft 18 when the dealer shows a Three through Six.

Player's cards   *Dealer's upcard*

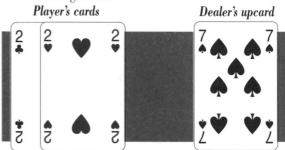

DOUBLE DOWN

Any other situation should be handled by the rules for standing and hitting.

SPLITTING PAIRS

Basic strategy guidelines for splitting pairs are uncomplicated as six easy-to-remember rules apply:

● Always split a pair of Aces or Eights.

Player's cards   *Dealer's upcard*

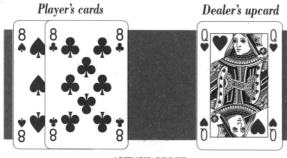

ALWAYS SPLIT

● Split Twos and Threes only when the dealer shows a Four through Seven.

Player's cards   *Dealer's upcard*

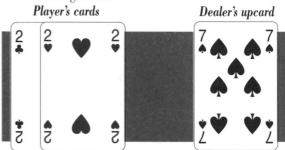

ALWAYS HIT, NEVER SPLIT

● Never split Fours, Fives or Tens.

Player's cards   *Dealer's upcard*

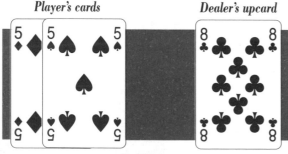

NEVER SPLIT

● Split Sixes when the dealer shows a Three through Six.

Player's cards   *Dealer's upcard*

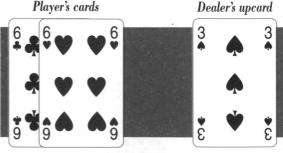

ALWAYS SPLIT

● Split Sevens when the dealer shows a Three through Seven.

Player's cards   *Dealer's upcard*

ALWAYS SPLIT

● Split Nines when the dealer shows Two through Six, Eight or Nine.

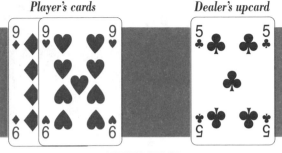

Player's cards   *Dealer's upcard*

ALWAYS SPLIT

BASIC STRATEGY vs CARD COUNTING

The other major blackjack strategy is known as card counting. In this system, the player keeps track of how many high cards remain in the deck. The theory is that high cards are good for the player. It's true that high cards are also good for the house, but through formulas developed by the Fifties mathematicians and computer programs written by today's experts, it was determined that players who count cards can actually gain a short-term advantage over the casino.

But because those situations don't occur that often, playing blackjack professionally can be a grind. Card-counting players must wade through hundreds if not thousands of hands before the odds turn in their favor. And then the counter measures employed by casinos may short circuit their chance to make any serious money.

For the recreational player, basic strategy makes much more sense. While the casual player doesn't play to lose, he also doesn't want to cram for an exam to enjoy a visit to a casino.

But the key to basic strategy is to stick to it; no going with a "feeling"; no "taking a shot". To be successful at basic strategy, you have to play it faithfully and approach the game confident that your basic strategy will be successful.

Misplaying hands will be the downfall of recreational players. Standing on a hard 12 against a dealer's upcard of Seven to Ace will cost players as much as 25 percent of the hands. Hitting a hard 15 against a dealer's Five or Six upcard costs just as much.

Doubling down on a hard eight against a dealer's Seven through Ace is a common mistake, costing between 25

percent and 60 percent of the player's bets. But a blackjack player who doesn't double down on a hard ten or 11 costs himself over 30 percent of his money.

Splitting cards is often an overlooked aspect of basic strategy. Players who neglect splitting can give away between 16 percent and 50 percent depending upon the dealer's upcard. If you've ever tried to split Tens at a blackjack table, it won't be long before you're playing alone.

Other players instinctively know that it is one of the worst moves. And the facts back them up. Splitting Tens can give away more than 50 percent of your bets, depending upon the dealer's upcard. Even against the Five or Six, the worst upcards for the dealer, splitting Tens costs nearly 20 percent of your bets.

The lesson is that basic strategy has proven to be the optimal blackjack strategy for recreational players. It gives you the best chance to beat the casino. When you go with a feeling or decide to take a shot, you're helping the casino, which certainly doesn't need your help.

THE NAME
OF THE GAME

Earlier in this chapter, you saw how rules can vary from casino to casino. But there are many other blackjack options that are offered in jurisdictions around the world.

Here are some favorable rules offered at some casinos:

● A five or six-card 21 is paid two-to-one;

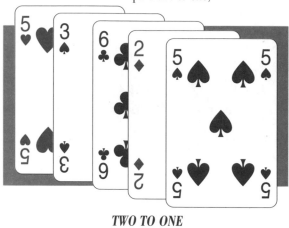

TWO TO ONE

● Three Sevens pays three-to-two;

THREE TO TWO

BASIC BLACKJACK STRATEGY

	PLAYER'S HAND	DEALER'S UP CARD									
		2	3	4	5	6	7	8	9	10	A
HARD TOTALS	5-6-7-8	H	H	H	H	H	H	H	H	H	H
	9	H	D	D	D	D	H	H	H	H	H
	10	D	D	D	D	D	D	D	D	H	H
	11	D	D	D	D	D	D	D	D	D	H
	12	H	H	S	S	S	H	H	H	H	H
	13-14	S	S	S	S	S	H	H	H	H	H
	15-16	S	S	S	S	S	H	H	H	H	H
	17-18-19-20-21	S	S	S	S	S	S	S	S	S	S
SOFT TOTALS	A-2(13), A-3(14)	H	H	H	D	D	H	H	H	H	H
	A-4(15), A-5(16)	H	H	D	D	D	H	H	H	H	H
	A-6(17)	H	D	D	D	D	H	H	H	H	H
	A-7(18)	S	D	D	D	D	S	S	H	H	H
	A-8(19), A-19(20)	S	S	S	S	S	S	S	S	S	S
SPLITS	A & A	SP	SP	SP	SP	SP	SP	SP	SP	SP	SP
	2 & 23 3	SP	SP	SP	SP	SP	SP	H	H	H	H
	4 & 4	H	H	H	SP	SP	H	H	H	H	H
	5 & 5 NS	D	D	D	D	D	D	D	D	H	H
	6 & 6	SP	SP	SP	SP	SP	H	H	H	H	H
	7 & 7	SP	SP	SP	SP	SP	SP	H	H	H	H
	8 & 8	SP	SP	SP	SP	SP	SP	SP	SP	SP	SP
	9 & 9	SP	SP	SP	SP	SP	SP	SP	SP	S	S
	10 & 10 NS	S	S	S	S	S	S	S	S	S	S

H=Hit, S=Stand, D=Double down, SP=Split, NS=Never split.

40

● Suited Six, Seven, Eight pays two-to-one;

TWO TO ONE

● Six-card unbusted hand wins;

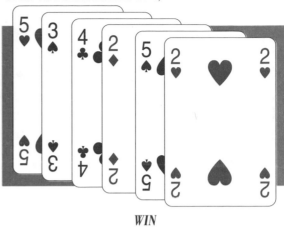

WIN

● Suited Ace, Jack pays two-to-one;

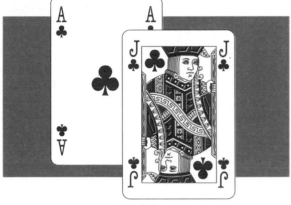

TWO TO ONE

● Suited blackjacks pay two-to-one;

TWO TO ONE

● Double on three cards or more;

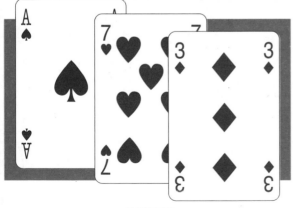

DOUBLE

● A 21 pushes a dealer's Ten-up blackjack;

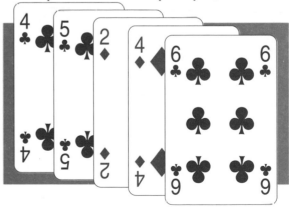

PUSH

● Triple Aces on split wins three-to-two.

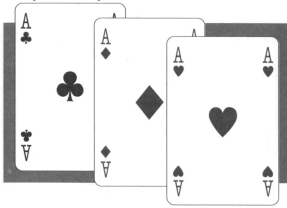

THREE TO TWO

To make blackjack more interesting, many casinos have developed variations or additional bets on blackjack games. In most cases, these varied and imaginative games should be avoided as they may distract beginning or intermediate players from their goal, which is to beat the house using basic strategy. But they can be enjoyable, once you understand that playing strict basic strategy is the only way to win.

Some of the more widespread blackjack options, that you will find in casinos around the world are:

● **Multi-Action Blackjack:** This game has three betting circles, in which you place three separate bets. The dealer uses one upcard, but plays it out three times to satisfy the three bets. The player plays out his hand before the dealer makes any moves. If he busts, he loses all three bets. Basic strategy should be used for this game, because the expectations are exactly the same. But the danger arises when the player doesn't make draws that may bust his hand, which plays right into the casino's hands. If you insist on playing this game, don't vary your basic strategy.

● Over/Under: In this game, you make a side bet on whether the next hand you will be dealt will be either over 13 or under 13 on the first two cards. Aces count as one, and the dealer takes all 13 ties. The rule is very unfavorable to the player, and should be avoided. But you can still play basic strategy blackjack on a table with this option without any effect.

● Red or Black: In this bet, you are wagering whether the first card you are dealt is red or black. This might appear to be a 50-50 proposition, but the casino throws in a kicker. If the second card is the same color as the one you choose, the bet is a push. Forget it.

● Face-Up or Double Exposure Blackjack: This game is not blackjack. Yes, you are trying to get closest to 21, but there's a considerable difference. You get to see both of the dealer's cards. Sounds good, doesn't it? Wrong. What you give up to see the dealer's cards simply isn't worth what you gain. You only get paid even money on blackjack, but the big giveback is that you lose pushes. There are situations, however, where the game can be played without giving the house an unreasonable advantage. But because it is rather extensive, it should be avoided until you feel comfortable with basic strategy to move on.

THE SYSTEMS APPROACH

WHICH SEAT IS BEST
AT A BLACKJACK TABLE?

Frankie plays blackjack almost every week. When he has a choice, he always sits at the last seat at the table, which is called third base. He doesn't like to sit at the first seat—first base—and be the first to get the cards.

Frankie prefers to see all the other cards come out before his cards. He's not a card counter, but all the same he gets certain "feelings" about which cards are coming next and third base is the perfect place for this.

What drives Frankie crazy when he doesn't sit at third base is when the last player takes the dealer's bust card. He never does that when he sits there.

Does it really matter whether you sit at first base, second base, or third base at the blackjack table? Your seat has absolutely no bearing on the natural order of how the cards come out in the shoe, so it doesn't matter.

Many players complain about how the third base player disturbs the order of the cards, by taking the dealer's breaking card. By sitting at the third base, or "anchor" position, they feel they can dictate what kind of card the dealer receives.

Is this logical? How can Frankie tell whether the card coming to him would be beneficial? He can't and he conveniently forgets it when his draw card would have busted the dealer.

Even a card counter wouldn't be able to know for sure whether a Ten or a low card was coming, and his play would be dictated by what's best for him, not what was worst for the dealer. If you've got a 15 and the dealer has 10, a Ten—value card coming would be detrimental to the third base player regardless of whether he drew it or the dealer drew it.

And one thing players tend to overlook is that the third base position will do as much to help the other players at the table as he will to hurt them. It just follows that the natural order of cards would not necessarily favor either player or dealer.

You can prove this for yourself. Keep track for a decent amount of time of how many times the third base player hurts the other players and how many times he helps them. You'll be surprised at what little effect the "anchor" has on the game.

But you'll never be able to convince Frankie.

CHAPTER 4

ROULETTE

FOLLOW THE BOUNCING BALL

Europe's most popular game, roulette, must be played precisely to provide a chance of winning. Despite a hefty house edge, players can find games that will be more favorable, and by using simple betting systems, they can beat the game.

Roulette players are often the most studious of all gamblers. You'll find them at the oblong roulette table hunched over a pad, carefully distributing their chips in a predetermined pattern only they understand. As the dealer spins the ball around the wheel, they stare at it as if their hopes and dreams can influence where the ball falls. When their bets are swept away, they turn again to the pad that only records where they've been, not where they're going.

FRENCH TWIST

The roots of roulette can be traced back to prehistoric China and the French monks. In the 17th Century, a French scientist, Blaise Pascal, who invented the first calculator, introduced a primitive version of roulette.

It wasn't until 1842 that Francois and Louis Blanc invented the single "0" roulette game. Ironically, the French brothers were forced to offer the game in Hamburg, Germany, since gambling was illegal in France at the time. The new game decimated the competition, which were offering an earlier version that featured higher odds. After Louis died, Francois was invited by the Prince of Monaco, Charles III, after whom Monte Carlo is named, to bring his game to the principality in southern France. Francois and his son Camille developed Monte Carlo into the world-famous resort we know today.

When roulette came to the US in the early 1800s, the Blancs's improvements were removed, and a double "00" returned. For a while, in fact, slick American operators added a triple "000", tripling the house edge and virtually ensuring that Americans would never warm to the game. The European game is today played in the great gambling palaces of Europe by tuxedoed men and elegant women in flowing gowns. It is especially popular with the ladies, who enjoy the glamor and relative simplicity of the game.

The black and red numbers are arranged in maddeningly random patterns that seem to suggest vulnerability. They aren't!

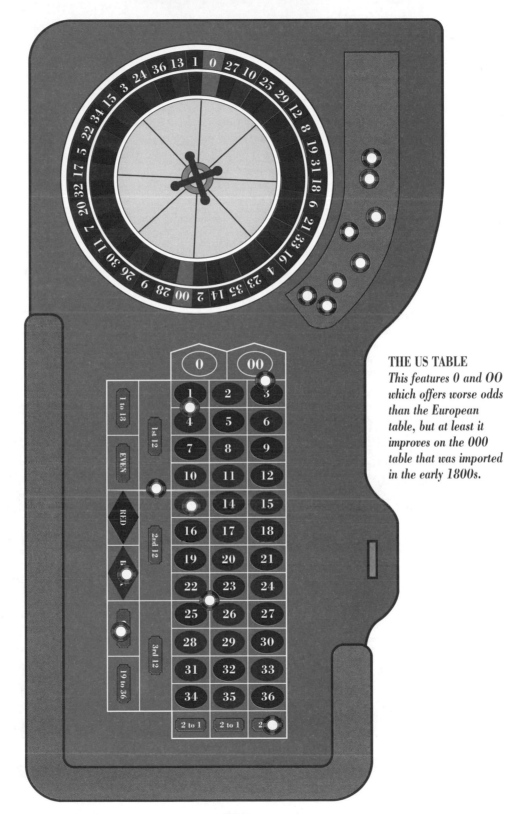

THE US TABLE
This features 0 and OO which offers worse odds than the European table, but at least it improves on the 000 table that was imported in the early 1800s.

TODAY'S REVOLUTIONS

Europe's most popular game never really caught on in the United States, perhaps because of the changes that the American casinos made to this glamorous game. While no longer having three zeros, with the extra "0", American roulette carries one of the heaviest casino advantages in the house, thereby discouraging the popularity it enjoys in Europe. With 38 numbers, players have to overcome a 5.26 percent house edge because whenever 0 and 00 are hit, all bets lose. This is over five times worse than playing the most favorable bets on the craps table, or utilizing blackjack basic strategy.

In Europe, roulette uses only 37 numbers—36 numbers and one "0." Even-money bets are placed "en prison" when 0 is hit. This is an option in which the player loses half the bet, or is permitted to let the bet remain in action, with the results to be determined on the next spin. Because the European version utilizes the "en prison" rule and

a single "0", the house edge is a comfortable 1.35 percent. The only American jurisdiction that offers "en prison" is Atlantic City, but because casinos there use 0 and 00, the house edge is halved to 2.7 percent. "En prison", or surrender, means that if the player has bets on the "outside"—odd/even, high/low, black/red, the dozens or the columns bets—he only loses half his bet when 0 or 00 hits.

Nonetheless, roulette remains an exciting game, mainly because of the variety of bets available. The 38 numbers in the American game are grouped into colors, columns and sections. The layout looks complicated, but is actually rather simple, once a road map is provided. Because roulette originated in France, and most European croupiers recognize bets made in French, we'll include the French translation.

OUTSIDE BETS

These wagers are placed "outside" the 38 numbers of the layout, and refer to specific sections or colors. The letters on the illustration correspond with the following bets:

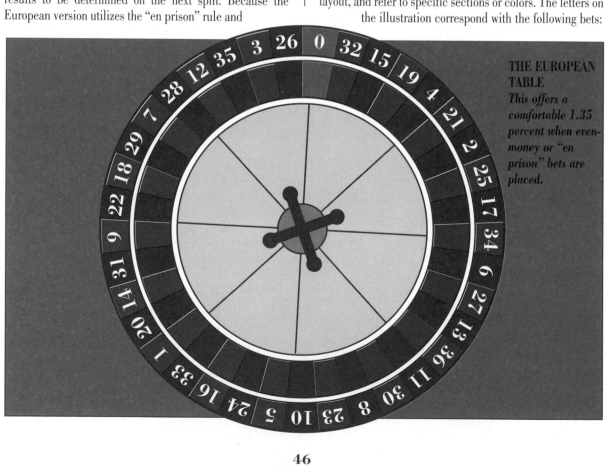

THE EUROPEAN TABLE
This offers a comfortable 1.35 percent when even-money or "en prison" bets are placed.

EVEN MONEY BETS

There are three even money bets. Chips are placed at the indicated locations and are on a one-to-one basis:

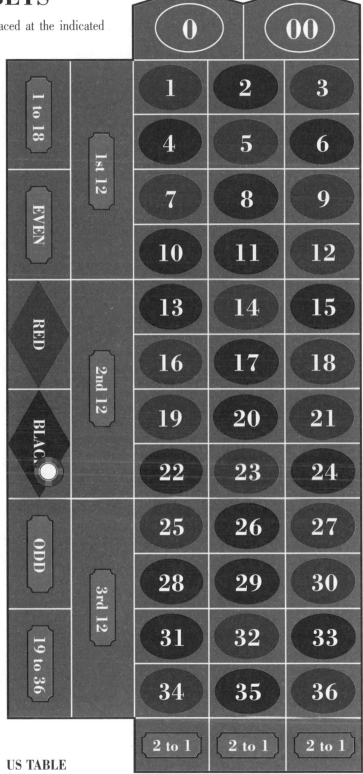

EUROPEAN TABLE

US TABLE

A) *Black and Red (Rougue et Noir): Players are betting that a particular color will come up, either black or red (in this case black). If either of the green numbers (0/00) come up, all bets lose, except as previously indicated, in Atlantic City.*

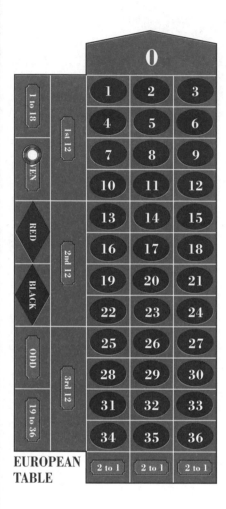

EUROPEAN TABLE

B) Odd and Even (Impair et Pair): Players are betting that the ball will land on one of the 18 odd or even numbers (even in this case).

US TABLE

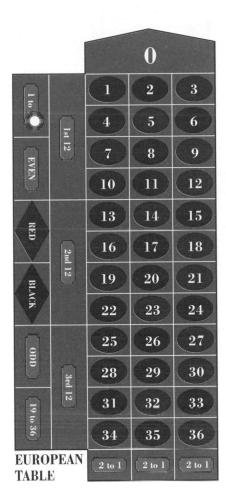

EUROPEAN TABLE

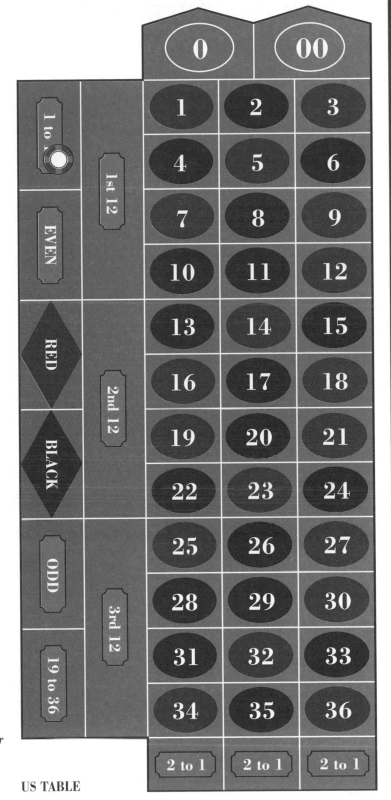

C) *High and Low, 1 to 18 and 19 to 36 (Passe et Manque): In this instance the player is wagering that the ball will land on one of the low numbers. At the opposite end the 19 to 36 bet is a wager on the 18 high numbers.*

US TABLE

TWO-TO-ONE BETS

Two bets on the roulette layout result in a payoff of two-to-one.

EUROPEAN TABLE

D) *Column Bets (Colonne): There are three columns of 12 numbers each. Bets are placed at the bottom of each column. Not included in the columns are 0 and 00.*

US TABLE

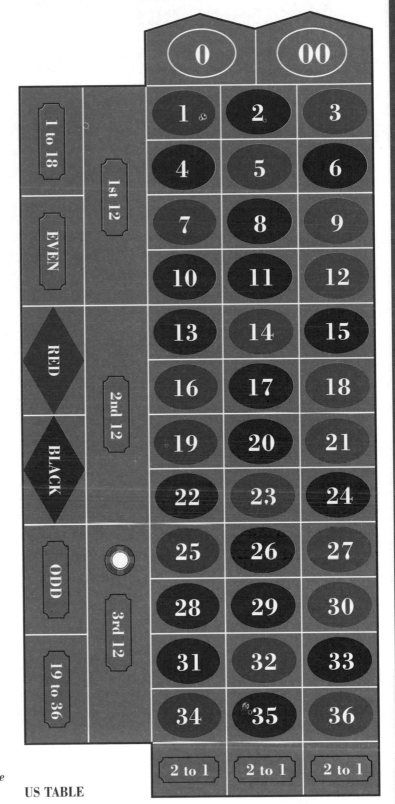

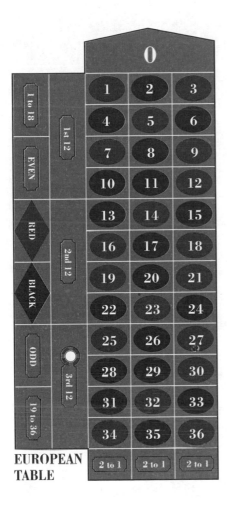

EUROPEAN TABLE

E) *Dozen Bets (Douzaine): There are three dozen numbers on the roulette wheel (not including 0 and 00). Bets are made alongside those dozen numbers.*

US TABLE

INSIDE BETS

The following bets are made either on the specific numbers or on the border of the numbers section of the layout. Payouts vary according to the amount of numbers bet.

EUROPEAN TABLE

F) *The Line Bet (Sixain): The player is betting that one of six numbers will come up. Bets are placed on the intersection of the two lines of three numbers. On the illustration, the bet will win if the numbers 31, 32, 33, 34, 35, or 36 are hit. The payout is five-to-one.*

US TABLE

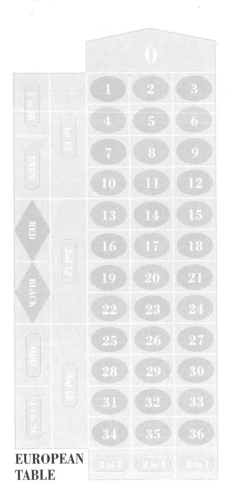

EUROPEAN TABLE

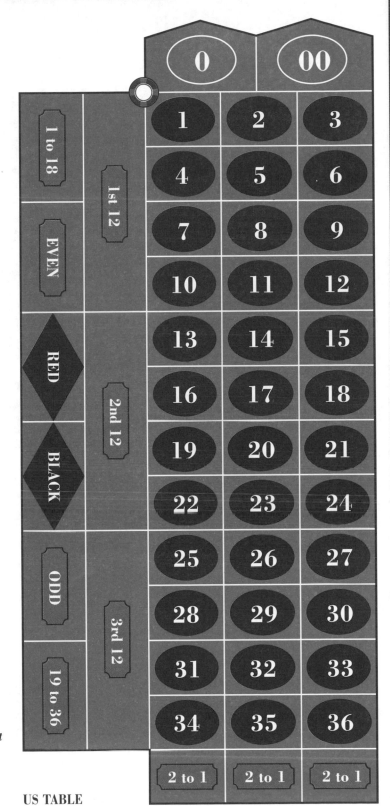

US TABLE

G) *The Five-Number Bet: There is only one five-number bet on the layout: 0, 00, 1, 2, and 3. The payoff is six-to-one. It is the worst bet on the table, with a house edge 50 percent higher than any other bet. This bet does not exist on the European game since there is no "00."*

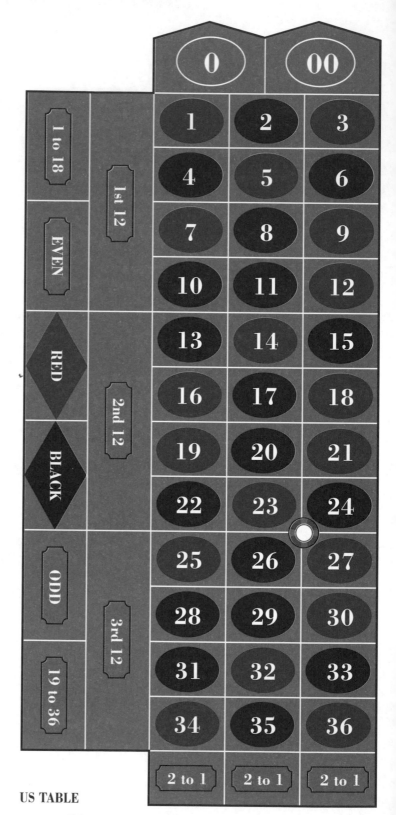

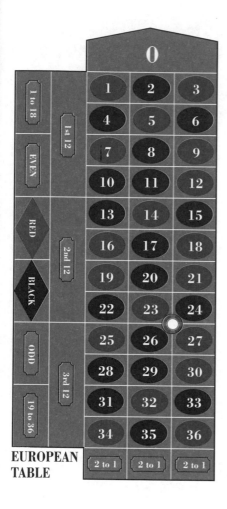

EUROPEAN TABLE

US TABLE

H) *The Corner Bet (Carre): Players are betting that one of four numbers will come up. Bets are placed at the intersection of the four numbers. On the illustration, a winning bet would get paid for the numbers 23, 24, 26, or 27.*

EUROPEAN TABLE

US TABLE

I) *The Street Bet (Transversale): Players are wagering that one of three numbers will come up. Bets can be made at several different places: at the end of the line (19, 20 or 21 on the illustration). A winning bet pays 11-to-one.*

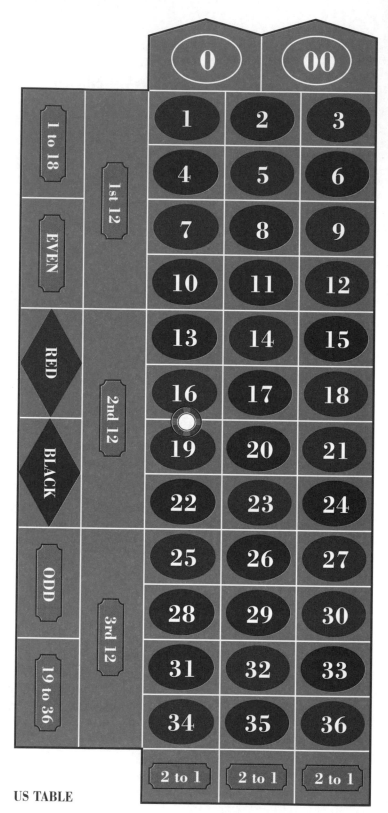

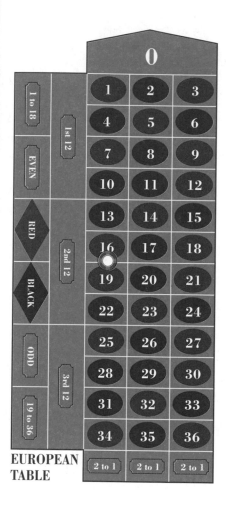

EUROPEAN TABLE

US TABLE

J) *The Split Bet (A Cheval): Players are betting that one of two numbers come up. Bets are placed to overlap the two numbers (16 and 19 on the illustration). Payoff is 17-to-one. The 0 and 00 bet can be made to overlap the two numbers or placed on the line separating the second and third dozen. It is the only bet that can be made at two places on the layout.*

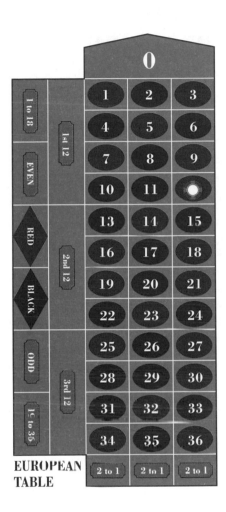

EUROPEAN TABLE

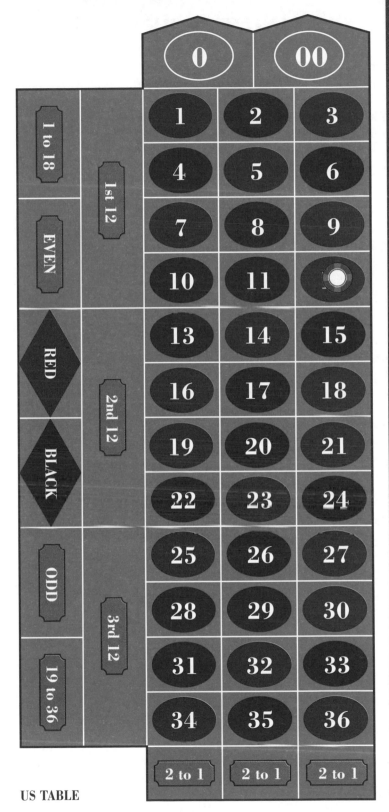

US TABLE

K) *The Straight-Up Bet (En Plain): The player is betting that one number will come up. Any number can be bet, including 0 and 00. On the illustration, the number 12 is a straight-up bet. The payoff is 35-to-one.*

PLACING THE BETS

Roulette is generally operated by two dealers. One takes all the bets, spins the ball, announces the number, takes all the losers and pays the winners. The second dealer, called a "mucker", re-stacks the chips and pushes the winning bets out to the first dealer who delivers them to the players. Frequently however, only one dealer handles all the action at the roulette table.

Once you understand how and where to make your bets, you begin by sitting down at the table and buying in. Please note that roulette is the only game in the casino that uses different, non-value chips. Although they are called non-value, that doesn't mean they don't represent money; they do. In this case, non-value means that they are worthless at any other gaming table, except at the specific table at which you are playing.

Check the minimums before sitting down. If you're playing a $5 minimum table, you must place at least $5 for every bet you make on the outside. For instance, if you are betting red, odd and the high bet (19-36), you must place $5 in chips on each bet. On the inside bets, however, your bets must only total $5. Whether you bet five numbers straight up, four numbers straight up and one split, or two corners, two split and one straight up, all your bets must total $5 or more.

Depending upon the minimum and your buy in, the dealer will ask you what value you want your chips to be. For a $5 game, the minimum value for chips is usually $1. For a $1 minimum game, chips will probably be worth 25 cents. It's generally your choice, and will be determined on how many bets you want to make on each spin.

If you are unsure of the procedures and the minimum bets at any table, simply ask the dealer, and he'll be glad to explain the casino's policy for roulette wagers.

These procedures vary in the European game. While American dealers sweep the layout with their hands and arms, European croupiers use a long stick, or "rake", to sweep in all bets. In Europe, roulette games do not use non-value chips. All players use the standard casino chips, which can cause great confusion when there are a multitude of bets on the layout. If you're playing in Europe, keep an eye on your bets and be certain how much you've bet. Bets are paid from the outside in. The dealer will pay the bets furthest away from him and work in, until he gets to the inside bets, which get paid last.

STROKING THE SYSTEMS

Beware of any roulette betting system that depends on a progression of bets, it is doomed to fail. You may experience some short-term wins with a progressive system, but eventually, the house advantage will catch up with you and you'll experience a disastrous loss that may wipe out any previous successful sessions.

Over the long run, any progressive betting system has to find a way to beat the hefty 5.26 percent house edge, and in the long history of roulette, no one has been able to develop a system that would beat even the low French disadvantage of 2.7 percent.

It becomes more important, therefore, to be able to rely on human or mechanical error to become a consistent winner at roulette. There are several "systems" that may help you discern where and when the ball is going to land in a particular number or group of numbers. By reading this next section, you will understand why many roulette players seem to be studying the wheel with such great concentration.

CLOCKING THE WHEEL

In most cases, you cannot predict where the ball is going to land, but many roulette players believe that by recording where the ball has landed in the past will allow them to estimate when it will land there again.

To accomplish this, roulette players sit for hours, recording the list of numbers that hit. They note when a number hits more frequently than should be statistically probable, and then wager on that number, hoping the trend will continue.

They will also try to determine whether the ball is landing in any one "section" more than another section. If you look at the roulette wheel and use the "0" as the 12 o'clock point, the wheel can be divided into four quadrants. The roulette wheel is masterfully laid out, even when the "00" is added. Directly across the wheel from any even number is the next odd number, and vice versa. Pairs of even numbers alternate with pairs of odd numbers, except when split by the "0" and "00".

Clocking the wheel can be very laborious, but some casinos have added an electronic device to help. These "scoreboards" record the last 20 numbers and colors that have it. For those who don't want to go back hundreds of spins, this scoreboard can be of great assistance.

One system is to note whether one or more numbers have hit twice or more within the last 20 spins. If so, the player places a straight-up wager on that number for the next five spins. If it hits, he pockets the profits and starts over. This continues until the number doesn't hit in five spins, and he gets up in search of another table hitting the "big" numbers.

Another method is to record the number of times the ball falls into a section of the wheel. By tracking the 20 spins, the ball must fall into one of the quadrants more than 25 percent of the time, since this should be the statistical norm. When you discover an anomaly, bet the numbers in that section for ten spins. If you win, continue to play that section until it regresses to hitting the normal amount, which should be five times for every 20 spins.

BIASED WHEELS

It is possible for a roulette wheel to be "biased" in such a manner that the observant player can obtain an advantage over the casino in the long run. These biases are caused by mechanical defects in the roulette wheel. But finding a wheel that is so defective as to actually overcome the built-in house advantage is extremely rare.

Most biased roulette wheels are not balanced correctly, and the spin of the wheel causes the ball to fall in one section of the wheel statistically more than in any other section. To make a valid observation, however, the player must be prepared to "clock" the wheel for an extended amount of time. The minimum amount of spins you want to observe is 500, because anything less would be considered short-term, and not statistically valid. You also must find a group of numbers that reoccur at least five percent more frequently

Use this table of "neighbors" to find sections to bet in.

SINGLE ZERO WHEEL									DOUBLE ZERO WHEEL								
12	35	3	26	0	32	15	19	4	30	26	9	28	0	2	14	35	23
5	24	16	33	1	20	14	31	9	29	25	10	27	00	1	13	36	24
15	19	4	21	2	25	17	34	6	25	10	27	00	1	13	36	24	3
7	28	12	35	3	26	0	32	15	26	9	28	0	2	14	35	23	4
0	32	15	19	4	21	2	25	17	1	13	36	24	3	15	34	22	5
30	8	23	10	5	24	16	33	1	2	14	35	23	4	16	33	21	6
2	25	17	34	6	27	13	36	11	3	15	34	22	5	17	32	20	7
9	22	18	29	7	28	12	35	3	4	16	33	21	6	18	31	19	8
13	36	11	30	8	23	10	5	24	5	17	32	20	7	11	30	26	9
1	20	14	31	9	22	18	29	7	6	18	31	19	8	12	29	25	10
11	30	8	23	10	5	24	16	33	7	11	30	26	9	28	0	2	14
6	27	13	36	11	30	8	23	10	8	12	29	25	10	27	00	1	13
18	29	7	28	12	35	3	26	0	17	32	20	7	11	30	26	9	28
17	34	6	27	13	36	11	30	8	18	31	19	8	12	29	25	10	27
16	33	1	20	14	31	9	22	18	10	27	00	1	13	36	24	3	15
3	26	0	32	15	19	4	21	2	9	28	0	2	14	35	23	4	16
23	10	5	24	16	33	1	20	14	13	36	24	3	15	34	22	5	17
4	21	2	25	17	34	6	27	13	14	35	23	4	16	33	21	6	18
14	31	9	22	18	29	7	28	12	15	34	22	5	17	32	20	7	11
26	0	32	15	19	4	21	2	25	16	33	21	6	18	31	19	8	12
24	16	33	1	20	14	31	9	22	21	6	18	31	19	8	12	29	25
32	15	19	4	21	2	25	17	34	22	5	17	32	20	7	11	30	26
20	14	31	9	22	18	29	7	28	23	4	16	33	21	6	18	31	19
36	11	30	8	23	10	5	24	16	24	3	15	34	22	5	17	32	20
8	23	10	5	24	16	33	1	20	0	2	14	35	23	4	16	33	21
19	4	21	2	25	17	34	6	27	00	1	13	36	24	3	15	34	22
28	12	35	3	26	0	32	15	19	19	8	12	29	25	10	27	00	1
25	17	34	6	27	13	36	11	30	20	7	11	30	26	9	28	0	2
22	18	29	7	28	12	35	3	26	12	29	25	10	27	00	1	13	36
31	9	22	18	29	7	28	12	35	11	30	26	9	28	0	2	14	35
27	13	36	11	30	8	23	10	5	31	19	8	12	29	25	10	27	00
33	1	20	14	31	9	22	18	29	32	20	7	11	30	26	9	28	0
35	3	26	0	32	15	19	4	21	33	21	6	18	31	19	8	12	29
10	5	24	16	33	1	20	14	31	34	22	5	17	32	20	7	11	30
21	2	25	17	34	6	27	13	36	35	23	4	16	33	21	6	18	31
29	7	28	12	35	3	26	0	32	36	24	3	15	34	22	5	17	32
34	6	27	13	36	11	30	8	23	28	0	2	14	35	23	4	16	33
									27	00	1	13	36	24	3	15	34

than would be considered normal in order to overcome the house advantage.

DEALER SIGNATURE

Dealers are human. They have friends and family, and lives outside of the casino. Not every dealer pays attention to his or her job 100 percent of the time. Because dealers may be thinking about other things while spinning the ball around the roulette wheel, the observant player may be able to determine whether that dealer is unconsciously (or consciously) giving the players an edge.

Some experienced roulette players swear that some dealers spin the ball at exactly the same speed each time. By noting where the wheel is at the exact moment the ball takes off, these players believe they can predict, within a few numbers, where the ball is going to land. Since you can continue to bet after the spin begins, they say they are able to cover those numbers and, more often than not, they claim to win. Skeptics discount these theories. Even if that were possible, they say, there are "ball stops" scattered around the wheel, little pieces of ornamentation that deflect the ball, making it difficult, if not impossible, to predict the ball's path.

Whether it works or not is debatable, but it's worth a look. Notice the speed of the ball as it leaves the dealer's hand. Count the number of times the ball circumnavigates the wheel. And, of course, note where it lands in comparison to where it was launched.

If you find a "dealer signature", it may only last for a short time. It could be at the end of the shift, when the dealer is thinking only about going home, or it could be at the beginning of the shift, when the dealer is thinking about the events of the previous evening. Like a human being, a dealer signature is a very fragile thing.

THE DECLINE OF ROULETTE

Casino executives, like all other businessmen, focus on the bottom line. Each game on the casino floor is expected to stand on its own. Complicated formulas tell executives how much each game is worth to the bottom line. Included in the equation are the costs for employees and equipment. In this context, slot machines are the best choice for the casino executives, with blackjack a distant second. Other table games, such as roulette and craps, barely register. A casino can generally make more money from three slot machines than from one roulette table. If promoted and managed properly, roulette could be a casino's most profitable game. To attract more action per hour to a roulette table, the casino must attract more players. But players are staying away from the tables in increasing numbers. Roulette has been described as a "sucker's game" over the past 20 years by virtually every gambling authority. Nobody wants to be thought of as a sucker and, as a result, roulette is ignored by serious players.

Another reason roulette is unpopular in the US is that the casino's attitude towards the players is often less than professional. Because of the house edge, casino executives know that roulette players don't have a chance, especially when they are uneducated about how to play. This causes casino executives to disdain roulette players.

It is that high house edge that accounts for much of the unpopularity. Why would anyone want to play roulette when there is craps (1.4 percent) and blackjack (0.5 percent with basic strategy)?

ROULETTE'S APPEAL

The disciplined non-professional player can expect to play with only a minor disadvantage in both craps and blackjack, but there is no escaping the 5.26 percent house edge in "00" roulette. But the vast majority of casino gamblers are playing for entertainment or excitement. Few are using a disciplined strategy that takes full advantage of any game. They are "hunch" bettors paying a big price for their long-shot play.

In blackjack, the hunch bettor will fall victim to a high house advantage. Since basic strategy can cut the house edge to a very attractive level, the opposite is also true. Players who bet with their hearts, instead of their minds, can raise the house edge to seven percent or more. Craps players are the same. Betting the field, the hardways, or the any seven bet may feel right at the time, but in the long run, you're damaging the overall appeal of craps, which is a low house advantage.

Because both of these games are touted as "player friendly", casino customers may not even realize they've dramatically increased the disadvantage they are facing by playing intelligently. But despite that these same players will avoid the roulette game, purely because they've heard of its high house edge.

Roulette is unique in that no matter how bets are placed, the house edge remains constant: 5.26 percent. This is still very high for even-money bets, but is a relative bargain for long-shot play. There is no other game in the casino which can offer up to a 35-to-1 payout with only a 5.26 percent "vig".

There is also no other game which does not penalize for hunch play. If you like to be entertained by hunch betting, and/or like to play for long odds on your hunches, then roulette is actually a much better deal than you'll find with either craps or blackjack.

FINDING THE RIGHT GAME

As you see, the only way to reduce the house advantage is to find a game that offers either surrender or a single "0" wheel. In the US, casinos go through phases of trying to attract the roulette player by replacing the double "OO" tables with some single "0" wheels. Whether it is Las Vegas or Atlantic City, those are the games you want to find.

But it depends on how you plan to bet. If you want to bet the big numbers, and go for the 35-to-one payoff, you want to find those single "0" games. But if you're more interested in betting the outside numbers, head for Atlantic City, where the surrender option cuts the edge on the outside bets to 2.7 percent. This doesn't help you on the inside, however, where the house edge remains 5.26 percent.

THE SYSTEMS APPROACH

THE THIRD WAVE
The layout of the roulette table is somewhat curious. The scattering of the numbers across the table have tempted players who are constantly in search of winning systems. One anomaly on the table has generated many system sellers down through the years who believe there is a sucker born every minute.

John is one of those "pushers" of a system that has been discredited for years. But the appeal of his argument is so strong, he gets at least a ten percent response whenever he finds a new list upon which to foist his sweet-sounding direct mail efforts.

The system is known as the "third column" system, and John is adept at explaining why it should work for you. Because the third column on the roulette table contains eight red numbers and only four black numbers, John reasons that it is a mathematical flaw that can be exploited by roulette players.

John believes that by placing a two-unit bet on black, which pays even-money, and a one-unit bet on the third column, which pays off at two-to-one, he will mitigate the

5.26 percent house advantage. With 18 black numbers in action and eight red numbers, he's reduced the prospect of losing to only the 12 remaining numbers (ten red numbers and the "0" and "OO").

John does very well when he lays this system out for his suckers...er, clients. "You're covered on 26 of the 38 numbers," he says. "How can you go wrong?"

Here's how. Let's run the math. For theoretical purposes, let's use 38 spins, one for each number on the roulette wheel. Let's assume that each number comes up once. Because you're betting three units for each spin, you've put 114 units in action (3 x 38).

By allowing each number to win once, when you've done the experiment, you'll have lost six units. That's six out of 114. Can you guess what that makes the house advantage on this bet? That's right, 5.26 percent.

John doesn't want you to do the math, and because of his winning manner, very few of his clients even question his system. But there's a loophole in every system. You just have to know where to look.

CHAPTER 5

BACCARAT

BOND...JAMES BOND

Baccarat is the casino's most elegant and profitable game, with an air of sophistication and wealth. Although it looks complicated and intimidating, baccarat is one of the casino's simplest and most profitable games for the player.

If roulette is a glamorous game enjoyed by Europe's upper crust, then baccarat is the game of kings. Until James Bond began playing the game in the 1960s, it was one of the casino's most misunderstood games. Couched in mystery, baccarat is conducted in a private gaming room, and caters to some of the world's biggest high rollers—or "whales" as they're known to casino executives.

The dealers are attired in tuxedos rather than standard casino uniform. The supervisors watch over the game like hawks, sometimes sitting in chairs elevated above the game, to give them a complete view of the action. The players seem to be a cut above those you'd find on the casino floor.

It seems a million miles from the rattle of the slots, where the players are noisily slamming coins into the shrill machines. Baccarat is unlike any other casino game, but it is in reality one of the simplest games in the house. But because of its elegant atmosphere, baccarat seems to be beyond the reach of the average gambler. Don't let them try to tell you that.

Baccarat (pronounced "bah-kah-rah") is one of the most socially involved games, one where you get to know your fellow players, and one where it's very difficult to do something wrong. At the same time, you can't make bad strategy decisions that will erode the minimal house edge. In short, baccarat should be investigated by any player looking for entertainment and a good return on their investment.

BACCARAT BACKGROUND

The allure of baccarat is one of the most historic of any casino game. It dates back to the middle ages, when the game was played with parts of a Tarot deck. It originated in Italy and migrated to France, where it became the game of the aristocracy.

Eventually, baccarat evolved into European baccarat and the French game chemin de fer (French for "railroad").

BACCARAT—THE HOUSE EDGE	
BET	*ODDS*
Bank	*1.17%*
Player	*1.35%*
Tie	*14.1%*

The Bank and Player bets are two of the best available.

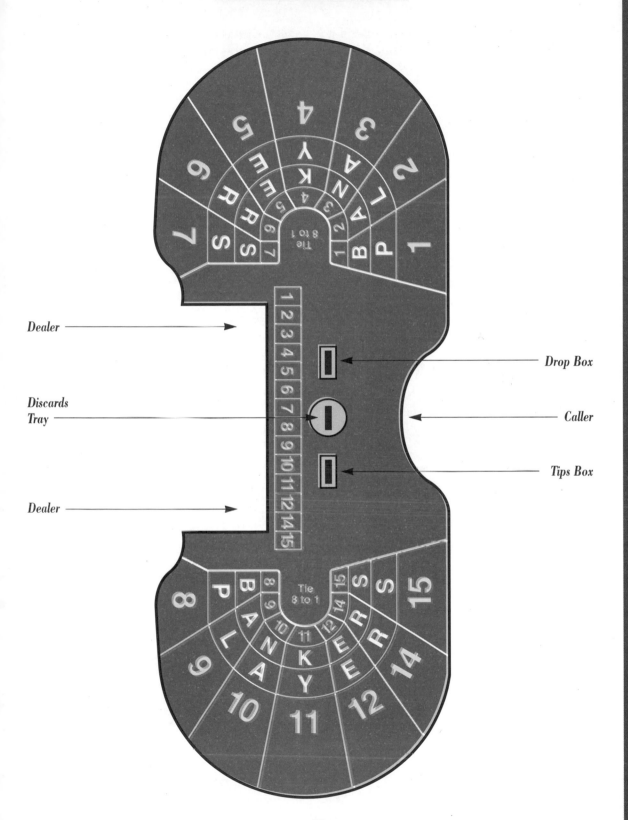

Dealer

Discards
Tray

Dealer

Drop Box

Caller

Tips Box

Each game gives the bank one slight rule variation that makes the game an even proposition for the casino and for the players. Chemin de fer is essentially the same game as today's casino game of baccarat, but one of the players banks the game, rather than the casino. The "banker" denotation rotates around the table. The casino takes no risk and merely charges a fee from each banker.

What is known as American baccarat actually originated in England and spread to South America. It was introduced into Las Vegas at the infamous Dunes casino in the late 1950s after Fidel Castro closed the even more infamous Havana casinos. Because it is so elegantly appointed, with

marble, chandeliers, plush chairs and more, you might think that baccarat is still the game of the aristocracy. You'd be right. Many of the world's highest rollers make it their game of choice. Stories abound about rich men—and women—who bet millions of dollars during one session. Casino revenues on the Las Vegas Strip rise and fall precipitously according to the casinos' fortunes at the baccarat tables.

There is a lesson to be learned by the choices made by these high rollers. They make their millions of dollars by making shrewd business decisions, and their choice of casino game reflects their understanding of the odds. Despite baccarat's elite reputation, the game is available to anyone who can

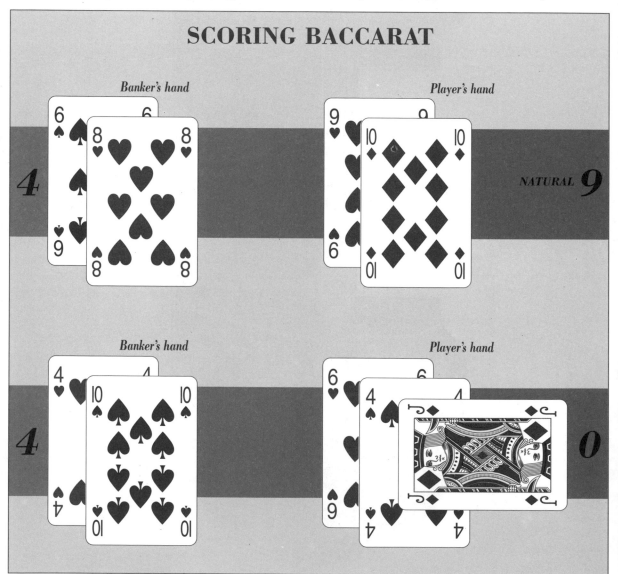

SCORING BACCARAT

make the minimum bet. In some cases, minimums can be as low as $5. At that level, a bankroll of $100 should be enough to truly experience one of the casino's most fascinating games.

While the game is enjoyed by people of many nationalities and ethnic groups, it is the Orientals that have made baccarat as popular—and profitable—as it is today. In some of the largest casinos in Las Vegas, several floors are reserved for large groups of Asians, who often spend many hours and even days playing their favorite game. Table maximums are a point of negotiation, and some groups and individuals can bet up to $500,000 a hand.

In the casinos of the Portuguese territory of Macao, near Hong Kong, baccarat is the game of choice, with dozens of customers lining up to play at a single table. These casinos allow more than one player to bet on a spot at the same time, while the dealers expertly track what each patron owes in commission on winning bank bets.

BACCARAT BASICS

Baccarat is a game with only two bets, banker and player. The odds are very nearly 50-50 for each and, as in most casino games, the deciding factor is most often nothing more than pure luck.

The baccarat table is oblong with seven numbered positions on each side of the table. Just like in hotels, the number 13 is skipped, so the numbers reach 15 at most games.

At each position there are three bets. The "Banker," the "Player" and the Tie. B-A-N-K-E-R and P-L-A-Y-E-R are spelled out on each side of the table in the corresponding areas. The position for the Tie bet is generally above the Banker and Player bets.

Three dealers work the games at all times and perform similar functions as the dealers at the craps table. Two dealers sit or stand behind the chip rack and pay or take the players' bets on each side of the table, depending upon the outcome of the hand.

A croupier, sometimes referred to as the "caller", stands in the middle of the table and makes the calls on the hands, directing the players on the procedures of the game. Baccarat is the only game where the players deal the cards.

Before starting the game, the dealers shuffle eight decks of cards together and place them in a covered shoe. Even the shuffling procedure is elegant. The croupier takes two decks off the top of the deck and "laces"—intersperses—them throughout the remaining cards. Player number one is offered the opportunity to be the "banker". As Banker, the player deals two cards for each hand. The first card is the first Player card, and goes to the croupier. The second card, the first Banker card, goes under the corner of the shoe. The third card, the second Player card, goes to the croupier, and the initial deal is complete with the fourth card, the second Banker card, which joins the first under the corner of the shoe. The croupier then passes the Player's cards to the player at the table with the highest bet on the Player's side. If no one is betting on the Player side, the croupier exposes the cards.

Players need not accept the shoe to act as the banker. It is not considered incorrect to pass the shoe, particularly if you plan to make a Player's bet. But you may take the shoe and bet the Player's side. Other players may comment that you're betting against yourself, but, once again, the rules are predetermined and the cards are already in the shoe, so it doesn't really make any difference what side you bet when you deal the cards.

The rules of the game determine whether a third card can be taken, but in the end, the winner is the hand with a total closest to nine. Face cards and Tens have no value and when the total of the cards is more than nine, the left hand digit is dropped. For instance, in baccarat, Eight and Seven equals Five, because you drop the ten-count of the true total of 15.

The only other bet that a player can make in baccarat is the Tie bet. It is a side wager that is usually placed along with a Banker or a Player bet. When a tie occurs, the two hands end up with the same total. Neither the Banker nor the Player loses and the casino pays the bets that were placed on the tie for that hand only. Ties pay 8 to 1, but the odds favor the house to such an extent, the tie wager is considered a bad bet.

Because the Banker bet has a slight advantage—the casino edge on the Banker bet is 1.06 percent versus 1.23 percent for the Player's bet—a winning wager on the Banker option owes the house a five percent commission. The commission raises the house edge to 1.17 percent. The dealer keeps track of your commission in a box in front of the chip rack by using plastic lammers designating the amount owed. You may pay this commission at any time, but it must be collected after the shoe is completed. Player bets are paid even money. The Tie bet is paid eight-to-one, but the true odds are more like nine-to-one, making the Tie bet the worst at the baccarat table.

After placing his bet, the Player has no more decisions to make. There are no double downs, splits, or free odds. The game proceeds according to a set of complicated rules that need not concern the casual player. With simple choices and clear cut decisions, the game is a real favorite with those gamblers who really like to rely on systems.

RULES OF THE ROAD

For those who want to understand the rules, baccarat is really rather simple. Since the object is to get the closest to nine, the perfect hand is one that totals nine in the first two cards. A face card and a Nine, a Seven and a Deuce, a Five and a Four…it doesn't matter. If it adds up to nine, you've got an unbeatable hand.

Eight is the second-best hand and, along with the nine, constitutes the two "natural" hands. They are each non-drawing hands—requiring no third cards. The only hand

SCORING BACCARAT

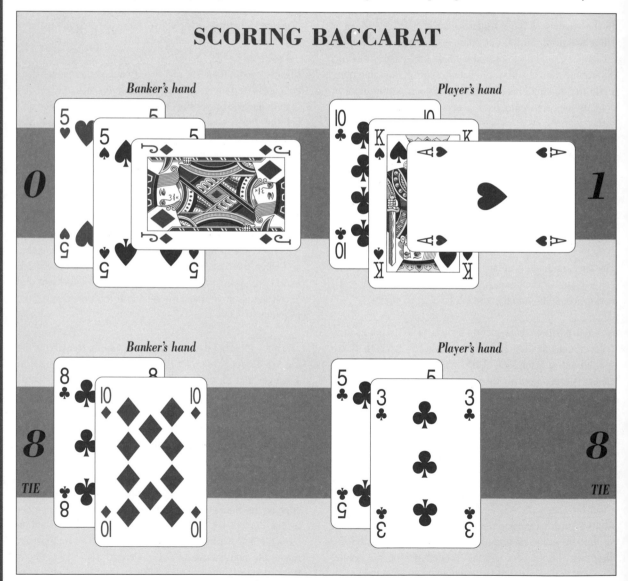

66

that will beat a natural eight is a natural nine. Each hand can, of course, be tied by one of the same value in the first two cards. If either the Player hand or the Banker hand has a natural eight or nine, the opposite hand cannot draw a third card, no matter what the value.

Each hand stands on seven, and the Player hand never draws on six.

The Player always draws when they has five or less (so long as the Banker does not have a natural eight or nine), and the Banker hand may draw on all hands from three through six, depending upon what the Player draws. Each hand always draws a third card when having two or less (three or less for the Player), so long as the opposing hand is not a natural.

This is where the rules get confusing. The Banker hand will draw on a six, when the Player hand draws a Six or a Seven. For example, let's say the Player hand totals three, and the Banker hand totals six. The Player draws first and if it draws a Six or Seven, the Banker hand must draw a third card. Even though a Seven would reduce the Player's hand to zero, the Banker is still required to draw, according to the rules.

The accompanying list, below, will explain the "third card rules" but, once again, it is not necessary to memorize these rules. The croupier will announce the results and rarely make mistakes.

If he does, there are at least six other people and surveillance employees observing the game. Don't worry you aren't going to get cheated.

The following are the third card rules for the Player's hand.
● The Player hand always draws on zero through five.
● The Player hand stands on six and seven.

The following are the third card rules for the Banker's hand. The Banker will draw if it totals:
● three, and the Player's hand stands on six or seven, or draws Ace, Two, Three, Four, Five, Six, Seven, Nine, or Ten.
● four, and the Player's hand stands on six or seven, or draws Two, Three, Four, Five, Six or Seven.
● five, and the Player's hand stands on six or seven, or draws Four, Five, Six or Seven.
● six, and the Player draws a Six or Seven. The Banker always stands if the Player stands on six or seven.

The difference between baccarat and chemin de fer occurs when the Banker has a five. In baccarat, the Banker is required to take another card under certain rules, but in chemin de fer, the Banker can decide not to take a third card under those situations.

KEEPING THE BACCARAT SCORE

Baccarat requires no skill. Luck is the dominant factor and nothing at all can be done to affect the outcome of the hand after you place your bet. All decisions are automatic. You cannot reduce the inherent house edge by altering your betting strategy or even counting cards. It's simply not possible.

A mathematical study of the game reveals that the Banker hand wins 45.8 percent of the time, the Player hand wins 44.6 percent, and the Tie wins 9.6 percent. By ignoring the tie bet, we find that the Banker hand wins 50.7 percent of the bets and the Player hands win 49.3 percent. The house charges the five percent commission because it would simply not be fair to give this sort of advantage to the baccarat player.

Like the toss of a coin, the hands in baccarat have no memory. Just as whether the previous coin toss came up heads or tails, it doesn't matter whether the previous baccarat hand is won by the Banker or the Player bet. You could toss ten heads in a row, and there's no guarantee the 11th would come up tails. The same is true in baccarat, but the "streak" of the same winning hand is what makes the game so fascinating.

Every casino provides a scorecard to its players to keep track of the winning hands. While this is a very useful tool, it's important to remember that it is simply a reflection of the "history" of the game. Many players believe that it is an indication of future trends, but many other players have gone broke trying to chase "patterns" or streaks.

Because baccarat offers simple decisions—odd-even, up-down, heads-tails—it is a game that has long intrigued systems sellers.

A simple system with a fancy name is the "Gargante Marche" system. In fact, this system is simply one that takes advantage of streaks. The theory is to latch on to a streak and ride it until it fizzles out. It sounds simple, but is actually difficult. While you're waiting for the streak in baccarat, you're going to experience what is known as a "chop", where the winning hand alternates between the Banker and the Player hands inconsistently. You'll be there for the streak, but you may have a long wait. In the long run, this system is no more effective than simply guessing which side is going to win.

One of the most famous—and most destructive—systems is called the "Martingale". It would be a perfect system, but is foiled by the casinos' insistence on a maximum bet. The object is to win one unit at a time. The Martingale system counts on the finiteness of streaks; that is, a streak always ends. In baccarat, the Martingale player would bet one unit on either the Banker or the Player bet. If he wins, he takes his one unit profit and leaves one unit as a bet. If he loses, he doubles his bet to two units. If he loses the two-unit bet, he makes a four-unit bet. If he loses the four-unit bet, he makes and eight—unit bet, and so on, until he wins the bet, making his one unit profit, and reduces the bet back to one unit.

The danger of the Martingale system is that you need to have a huge bankroll and be ready to risk it for a reward of only

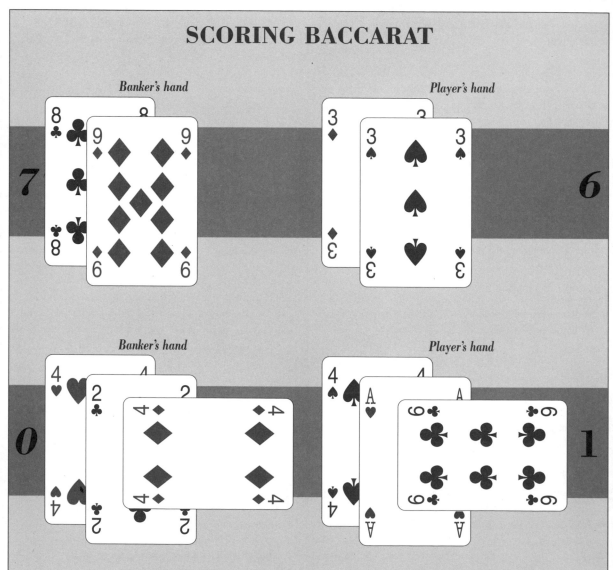

SCORING BACCARAT

Banker's hand   *Player's hand*

Banker's hand   *Player's hand*

one unit. In a $5 minimum baccarat game that would generally have a maximum of $2,000, a streak of ten would wipe out the Martingale player to the tune of over $3,000. That's a lot to risk for a $5 win.

More typically, a baccarat game carries a $20 minimum, and a $4,000 maximum. In that case, it only takes a streak of seven to induce "gambler's ruin".

An 18th Century French mathematician thought he had devised the perfect system. Jean Le Rond d'Alembert reasoned that when two events have an equal chance of happening—as with the two hands at baccarat—if one

begins to happen more frequently than the other, the alternative event must eventually begin to occur more often in order to even up the odds, or achieve equilibrium. Nature always seeks equilibrium, d'Alembert believed.

In the d'Alembert system, the player bets one unit on either the Banker or Player. When he loses, he increases his bet by one unit. When he wins, he decreases his bet by one unit. Bets will vary according to size, but eventually he will find himself betting one unit, and equilibrium will be achieved. Losses will be balanced by an equal number of wins. The problem with this system is that it is simply hogwash. Nature does not try to achieve equilibrium. Baccarat has no

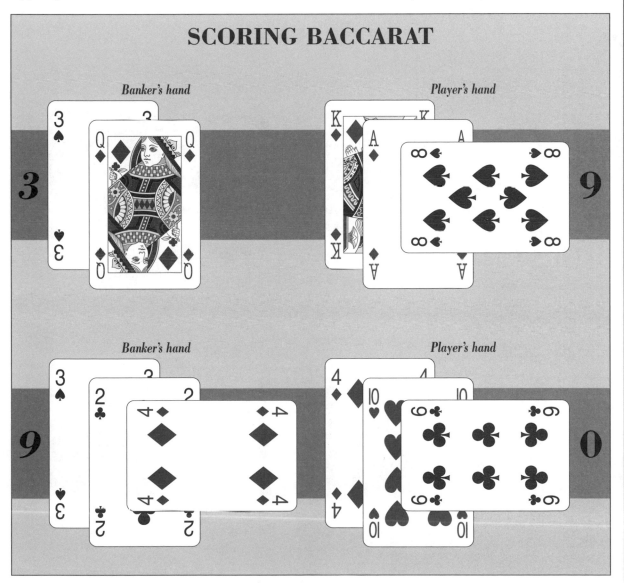

SCORING BACCARAT

memory, so the result of one hand or a series of hands do not affect the next one or the next series. Just because the Banker hand won ten in a row doesn't mean that the Player hand will win ten straight anytime soon. In fact, the difference could even get larger. In the long run, the ratio of Banker hands to Player hands may get smaller, but the difference between the number of hands could actually increase in the short run.

OK, so you see the d'Alembert system is destined to lose. So why not do the exact opposite. Since the Martingale system will lose, let's try the reverse. This can be applied to many systems, but unfortunately, the logic doesn't hold up. You

see, any system is irrelevant. Players lose because the loss is only a combination of the amount wagered with the house edge. It's impossible to defeat the house edge. In the long run, the player would lose just as much money by betting one unit at a time, as he would by utilizing one of the above systems. A system may only alter the size and times of the wins or losses; for instance, many small losses and a few large wins.

While some so-called experts have developed complicated card counting systems for baccarat that favor the Banker or Player, they still do not reduce the house advantage. There is, however, one perfect bet in baccarat which is guaranteed

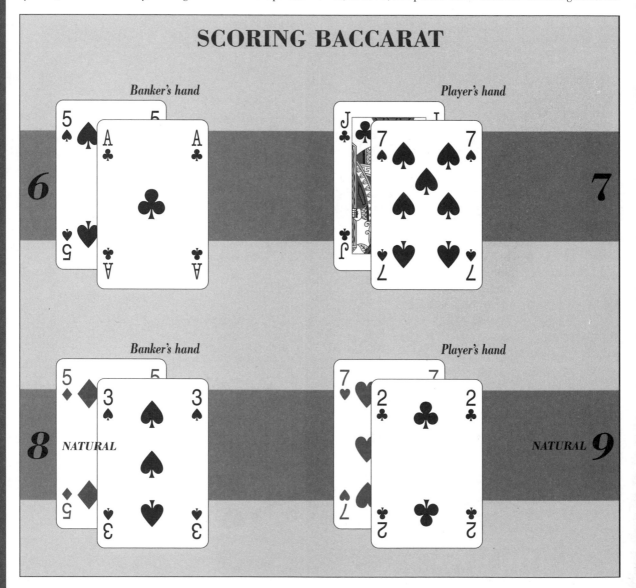

SCORING BACCARAT

Banker's hand

Player's hand

6

7

Banker's hand

Player's hand

8 NATURAL

NATURAL 9

to win that involves card counting. It was developed by a baccarat supervisor in Atlantic City in the late Seventies, but is so rare, you'd have to play hundreds, perhaps thousands, of games before it appeared.

The baccarat shoe is dealt nearly to the end and the players see every card. When loading the shoe, the croupier counts a cushion of 10 or 15 cards from the end and places a yellow card at that spot, that guarantees enough cards for one more hand after the yellow card appears. Since Tens and face cards are worth nothing in baccarat, this supervisor suggested that if you could count all the cards that are dealt in baccarat and determine that all the cards remaining when the yellow card appears are Tens or face cards, you know a nothing-nothing Tie will be declared on the last hand.

A player with that knowledge would then place the maximum bet on the tie—$500 at that time—and sit back and collect his winnings. With an eight-to-one payoff on the tie, this bet would garner a $4,000 payout. The problem is

that the odds of the final 10 or 15 cards all being Tens or face cards are pretty high. But all in all, it's not bad for a perfect bet!

THE SMALL GAME

As we've seen, since the middle ages, baccarat has been considered the game of the rich. When it was introduced into Las Vegas, casino managers tried to maintain that aura, and succeeded beyond their wildest imaginations. High rollers from around the world today visit Las Vegas to experience the game in its most luxurious settings.

Other casinos saw the success with the high rollers and tried to interest the rank-and-file gambler in the game in order to expand its appeal (and to make more profits, of course). In order to put it within reach of most gamblers, mini-baccarat was invented. It is essentially the same as the big game, but played at a blackjack-sized table. It's the generic version of the game, but with all the fabulous and highly enjoyable

MINI BACCARAT

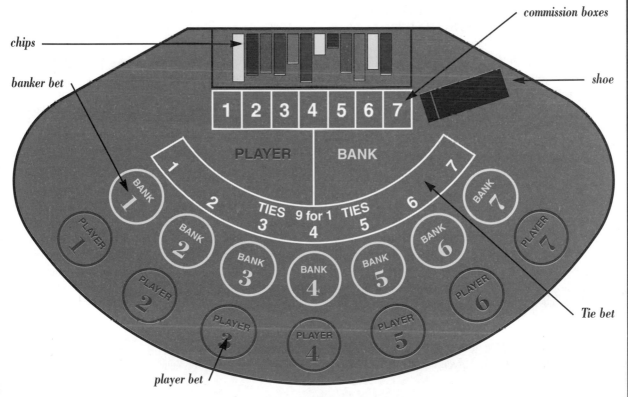

accoutrements stripped away. Like blackjack, it seats seven players. Each player has three spots, the Banker, Player and Tie bets. The game is conducted by a single dealer. The players do not handle the cards in mini-baccarat.

The dealer draws the cards according to the same rules as the big game. Winning Banker bets are charged the same five percent commission and the house advantage is the same, as well.

The only difference between the two styles of baccarat is the speed of the game. At the large game, only two, maybe three, hands can be dealt per minute. At mini-baccarat, five, sometimes six, hands can be dealt per minute.

As the tempo of the game increases, the house gets more shots at your money. Even though the house edge doesn't change, if there are more decisions per hour, you're going to lose at a faster pace. But since the minimums are lower, you'll lose less than at the larger table. Mini-baccarat is a good way to learn how to play baccarat without losing more than you'd like. It's also a good game for anyone who wants to play a simple game that requires no playing strategy.

But bear in mind that for all the similarities with the big game, mini-baccarat is not baccarat. The elegance and appeal of the big game is worth spending the extra time and investing the money on. You'll get attention normally reserved for the high rollers, and feel like one, as well.

THE SYSTEMS APPROACH

BETTING BACCARAT

Reba sits quietly at the baccarat table, fingering an old, worn silver dollar her father had given her many years ago. Though she loses more often than she wins, she still considers the coin her lucky charm. Tonight, it is working. She has won five consecutive bets.

The shoe containing the cards is offered to her. She pulls the shoe close to the rail and suddenly flips the silver dollar. She watches intently as it lands, heads up, on the green felt layout in front of her. Sliding several chips up to the area designated "BANKER", she proceeds to deal herself another winner. This is a rather unorthodox and less than scientific system but it serves her well.

Baccarat is a game of streaks. Whether it is several Bank hands in a row or many Player hands, money is made by pressing the advantage at this time. The best and simplest method to take advantage of these streaks is called "following the shoe". This simply means that you bet on the side that won the previous hand. If the Bank won the last time, you bet the Bank. Using this system, you will never miss a streak no matter which side is doing the winning. The major drawback is that when the winners occur in an alternating, back-and-forth pattern, called a "chop", every hand is a loser.

The system used to defuse that problem is called the "Every Other" method, where instead of betting the winner of the previous hand, you bet the hand that won

two hands ago. For instance, if the shoe started with a Bank winner and then a Player, on the third hand you would bet the Bank, since it won two hands ago. The fourth hand, you would bet the Player, for the same reason. Using the "Every Other" system enables you to avoid the chop while taking advantage of the streaks inherent in baccarat. Of course, and extended period of two wins in a row by each side will rapidly deplete even a high-roller's bankroll.

As with every system, money management is an important consideration. With the "Follow the Shoe" and "Every Other" system, the player bets the minimum unit and presses the bet when they win. But baccarat is not for the faint-hearted. The following systems are not recommended for those with a limited bankroll, because they force a player to "chase his money"— that is, to double up after a losing bet to re-capture their losses. But these are some of the reasons high rollers like baccarat.

A MARTYR TO MARTINGALE

He looks a little bit like W C Fields, with a bulbous nose and bulging stomach. George seems more interested in entertaining the supervisors, dealers and players than in playing the game. But everyone knows that he is deadly serious about baccarat. His system has won him money almost daily, though sometimes it is an uphill battle.

It is a simple system, based on the theory that the Bank hand will not go for very long before it wins two in a row.

George will bet his minimum unit—in his case, $100—after a Bank win. He is hoping for a repeat. If he wins, he will pull all his money off and wait until a Player win interrupts the Bank cycle. He will then make another $100 bet after the next Bank win. If he loses that bet, he will again wait for the Player interruption and double his bet after the next Bank win. He will continue to double his bet until the Bank does repeat.

The casinos have table maximums to prevent this type of system, but George rarely has to go that far. This time, however, George is in trouble. He has reached the point where he cannot double his bet, because of the table maximum. He is forced to bet in reduced units that will require two or three separate wins, before he gets even. His friendly and casual conversation disappears until he finally wins the last bet, when he decides to take a break, obviously relieved.

THE STATISTICIAN

Mickey is a bit more analytical than George, though his personality is even more extravagant. Each time he plays, he is accompanied by different young ladies, who appear to be a third of his age. His outlandish style of play makes him the center of attention.

He has kept all of his baccarat scorecards since he began playing, years ago. Using a computer to help him diagnose trends, he has determined the odds on lengthy streaks, discovering that long streaks mean equally long odds. To get the jump on the shoe, Mickey will make large bets—$500 to $2,000 —on runs of two and three hands in a row. He will then begin to decrease his bets, knowing that the longer the streak lasts, the less chance it has of continuing.

Unfortunately, Mickey did not have the discipline needed to stick to his system. He was more interested in impressing his lady friends than turning a profit. Today, Mickey has depleted his once—impressive bankroll and is but a shell of his former self.

SYSTEM SUCCESS

The systems mentioned above are but a few of many methods developed for baccarat. Since baccarat is one of the oldest, most established of the casino games, it has been thoroughly analyzed and dissected. If a foolproof system had ever been developed, outside of cheating, the casinos would have figured out a way to stop it.

Systems are methods designed to improve your chances of winning. Most systems require an established bankroll that depends upon table minimums and the player's wallet. Discipline is as important as money, however. But the key ingredient in any casino decision is the enjoyment of the player. The best system for one player may not work for another. If you're comfortable with the system, it works for you!

Silver dollars, anyone?

CHAPTER 6

CRAPS

THE DICE DILEMMA

The most exciting game in the casino is undoubtedly craps. Most of the shouting and rooting can be traced to the dice games, and for good reason. Craps can be the most favorable game in the casino if you understand how to take advantage of its attractive bets.

Blackjack players approach their game with the studiousness of a professor. Roulette players are like cartographers, mapping their way around the multi-numbered layout. Baccarat players are serious gamblers, with their emotions riding the game's twists and turns. And slot players stare at their machines with a mind-numbing expression, only breaking their rhythm to quickly celebrate a win or get more coins.

But over in the corner, you hear some yelling and rooting, it seems like the most exciting place in the entire casino. You see a crowd of people gathered around what appears to be a pit, but is actually a craps game. Craps, or dice, is easily the casino's most thrilling game. When the dice are falling the right way, there are few other experiences that rival the camaraderie that the players feel at that table. As the shooter rolls number after number (but no seven, please), craps can be exhilarating, and more importantly, it can be profitable.

But craps can also be the most frustrating of all casino games. Because to play craps successfully, you have to understand how to place and decipher a wide variety of bets. It's therefore important to stay alert and positive. Needless to say, that is rarely possible when every other roll is a "Seven out"!

SIMPLE, YET COMPLICATED

Because the table layout has multiple areas in which to place bets, and the amount and payout of those bets vary, modern players have abandoned craps to concentrate on simpler, less confusing games. But those players are missing out on one of the last bastions of true gambling.

The activity at a craps game is very confusing to a novice. Players throw chips to the dealer yelling what seems to be a secret code, such as "Give me a hard eight for five," "C and E for a deuce!" "I'll take a two-way yo."

It's easy to see why observers are mystified by this repartee, but many of these bets are ones that the knowledgeable craps player will not make. Many people play craps, but very few play it skilfully, and there lies the difference in a game that wins a great deal of money for the house, but at the same time, treats the intelligent player very well.

To understand why the house makes so much money at the craps table, you first have to understand why. There are only so many ways to roll specific numbers on the two dice you use in craps. For instance, there are only two ways to roll the two or 12. The true odds of that occurring are 35 to one. But the casino does not pay off your bet at the correct ratio, for the two or 12, you only get 30 to one. That gives the casino a rather hefty house advantage of nearly 14 percent on that bet. So you see, when the house takes such a big percentage of what you're supposed to get on that bet, the intelligent craps player will avoid those bets. Later on in this chapter, we'll review the bets you should not make on a craps table.

THE BASICS

You don't just walk up to a craps table and begin to play. That is the main reason that craps is a "dying" game in the casinos. Where it once dominated the American casino, craps is now disappearing, as the players who learned the game in the back alleys of the major cities, or the barracks of the armed services get older and disappear. But for those who want the best action in a casino, craps is the only game to play.

Let's start by looking at the craps layout. Confusing, right? It's true that there are dozens of bets available to the craps player, but intelligent players will ignore a majority of those bets and concentrate on those that give you the best chance to win. So for the moment, we're going to forget about the pie-in-the-sky bets and concentrate on how to get started.

Don't walk up to an empty game to play, because although the odds are no different at an empty table than at a full table, you won't get the flavor of the game without at least a few players. But in contrast, don't try to get into a game that is jam-packed with players with a lot of hootin' and hollerin' because no one will want a novice who might slow up the rolls of the "hot" dice.

Pick a calm game with a few players and plenty of room to spread out. Tell the dealer you're just getting started. Most dealers who aren't too busy will take the time to walk the novice through the game, explain the different bets and the procedures. They understand that their livelihood as craps personnel depends on developing the new players.

A craps table employs three dealers at a time: two stand behind the table to accept bets and to either pay off winners or take down losers. On the other side, in the middle of the table, is the stickman, who handles the dice with a "stick" and controls the speed of the game. Sitting down opposite

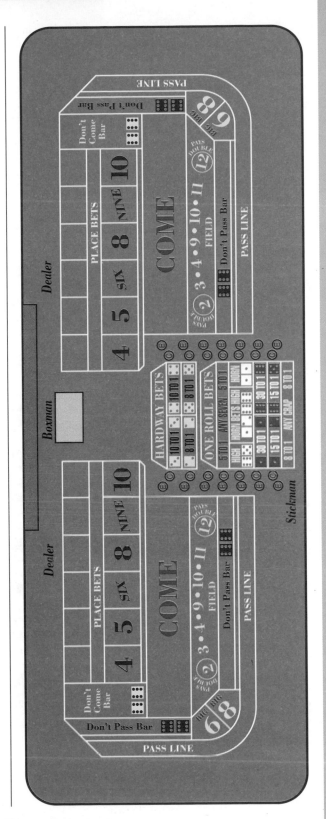

the stickman is the boxman, who acts like a supervisor in blackjack, approving all buy-ins and large payoffs.

Here's the secret of the simplicity of craps. On the first roll of the dice—the "come out roll"—the stickman will slide five dice to a player—the "shooter"—who will then select two dice. He'll throw the dice to the opposite end of the table. The dice must hit the wall of the table to be considered a legal roll.

The shooter tries to establish a number—four, five, six, eight, nine or ten. The dealers will then take a "puck" that says "off" on one side and "on" on the other side, and place it on the number rolled, "on" side up—it is always "off" on

the come-out roll. The shooter will then attempt to roll that number again before he rolls a seven. And that's the entire objective of craps.

Other things can happen, of course. Normally, the shooter places a bet on the "pass line". When they roll that number again before rolling a seven, they have made one "pass". When you bet on the pass line, the "front line", you're betting on the "do's" or you're betting "right". Most players bet the pass line because it means they are going "with" the shooter, hoping that he gets a pair of hot dice and rolls all night. When you're betting on the "don't pass" line, you're betting on the "don'ts" or you're betting the "wrong" way. The players who bet the don't pass line believe that the

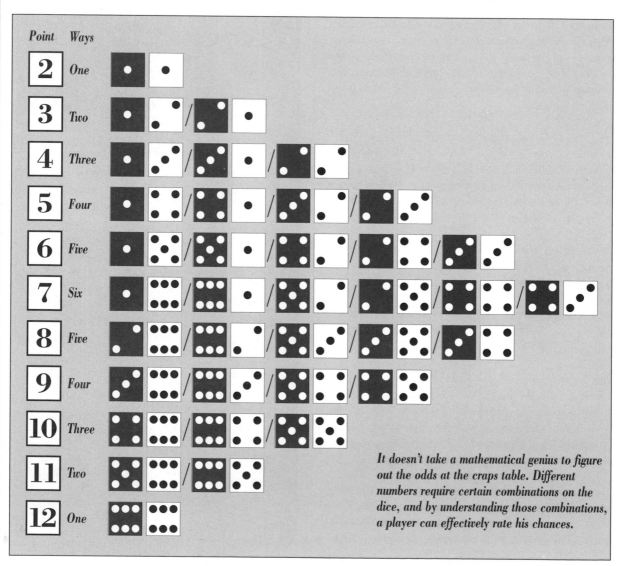

It doesn't take a mathematical genius to figure out the odds at the craps table. Different numbers require certain combinations on the dice, and by understanding those combinations, a player can effectively rate his chances.

odds of rolling a seven will eventually catch up to the shooter, and they want to profit from those odds.

If the shooter rolls a seven or 11 on the come-out roll, he wins. The stickman may say, "Winner, front-line winner, pay the do's, take the don'ts." The don't bettors lose their money, and the shooter continues to roll.

If the shooter rolls a two, three or 12 on the come out roll, he loses. The stickman will most likely say, "Two (three or 12). Craps, line away. Take the do's. Pay the don'ts. 12 is barred. (If the 12 shows, the pass line bettors lose, and the don't pass bettors don't win or lose, they get a push.) If the shooter "craps out"—rolls his point and then rolls a seven—he passes the dice to the next shooter.

When the shooter establishes a point, say a six, the stickman will announce "Six, mark the six." The shooter will then have a chance to roll again to try to make a six before he rolls a seven. If he makes his point, he gets a chance to establish another point. He will continue to roll until he rolls a seven, when he'll "seven out".

And this takes us to the next level, the most profitable step, in a craps game.

FREE ODDS

Take a look at the layout again. In some casinos, you'll see a "Big 6 and 8" at the corner of the table and a large area to make "field" bets. The "hardways" and "one-roll" bets virtually shout out to you with their dice diagrams. Forget all them. They're like billboards for bad bets, and the casino would love you to make those bets on every roll.

The best bet on the dice table isn't even printed on the table. The best bet on the table is the "free odds" that you get to place behind your pass line bet. Pass line bets are paid at even money. If you bet $5 on a shooter and he rolls a six as the point, and makes that six, the dealer will pay you $5 for your pass line bet. The house has a small advantage of 1.4 percent on pass line bets.

You can reduce that edge substantially by putting up free odds, an additional bet that gets paid off at the true odds of the number rolled. Let's say you bet $5 on the pass line, and the shooter rolls a four. The odds of rolling a four are two-to-one, but you only get even money on the pass line. But if

you take free odds, you get paid two-to-one for your free odds, because there are only three ways to make a four, while there are six ways to make a seven.

The ten and four are called "sister" numbers because the true odds of rolling a four and ten are the same. Other sister numbers are the six and eight, and the five and nine. The free odds are more complicated for these numbers.

When you roll a six, there are five ways to make a six, while we've seen there are six ways to make a seven. So if you have a $5 bet on the pass line, and back that up with $5 in free odds, and a six is rolled, you'll get paid $5 on the pass line, and $6 on your free odds, for a total payoff of $11. The same is true for the eight.

Now the five and nine are a little more complicated. There are four ways to make the five or the nine. So true odds are six to four, or three to two, or nine to five.

If you win a $5 bet on the pass line, and you place a $5 free odds bet behind the line, you should get paid $7.50. But you won't because the casino doesn't want to deal in coins. To get the full advantage of your free odds on the five and nine, you're going to have to add $1 to your free odds, to increase your free odds bet to $6. If you do that, the dealer will give you $9, making your total payoff $14 for risking $11.

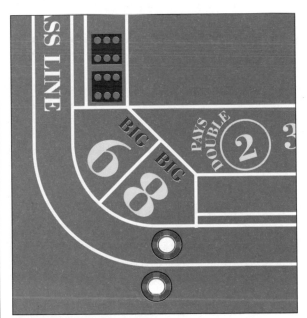

Free odds can be taken by placing one or more chips behind your pass line bet.

By taking these free odds, you've reduced the house edge on the pass line to less than one percent, clearly the best bet in the house.

In most casinos, you may reduce your edge even further, because the majority of gaming halls allow you to take at least double odds. That means, for the four and ten, you can bet $10 in free odds behind your $5 pass line bet. Should a five or nine be rolled before a seven, the dealer will pay you two-to-one on your free odds and even money on your pass line bet, for a total of $25 for $15 risked.

Because there is a dwindling pool of craps players, casinos in major jurisdictions value their loyal customers. If they didn't have excitement at their craps games, the game would eventually disappear in individual casinos, severely impacting the bottom line. So many casinos use odds as a marketing tool. In some places, you can get triple, quintuple and even ten-times odds at the craps game. These promotions are very valuable to intelligent players. In some casinos in Tunica, Mississippi, in 1995, craps games were offering the unheard-of 20-times odds.

Understand, however, that while the casino has no house advantage on the free-odds bet, you must risk more money than your original bet to win. And even though there is no house edge, the chances of winning or losing the bet is right down the middle, 50-50. If you've got a small bankroll, and take double odds on your $5 line bet each time, you could be in trouble if you hit a losing streak. It doesn't take long to lose your entire stake, even if you are playing even with the house.

You may not remove pass line bets until they are resolved one way or another, but you may remove odds bets at any time. Since the casino would prefer you don't take odds to begin with, it will allow you to remove them whenever you want. Don't do it.

COME ALONG

To get the most advantage out of craps, you should make multiple bets on different numbers. There are a variety of ways to place these bets, but one of the simplest is the "come line". The come line is the same as the pass line. It's betting the do's and backing the right bettors. You can only place the come bet, however, after a point has been established.

Let's say you have a $5 bet on the pass line, and the shooter established four as the point. Take another $5 chip and place it on the come line. There are now five results that can occur on the next roll.

● The shooter rolls a seven. You lose your $5 pass line bets, but you win $5 on the come line.
● The shooter rolls an 11. You win your $5 come line bet, and the pass line bet remains.
● The shooter rolls a two, three or 12. You lose your come line bet, but the pass line bet remains.
● The shooter rolls a four. You win your pass line bet, and the come line bet is moved to the place bet box four, and becomes a separate bet that will only be resolved when a

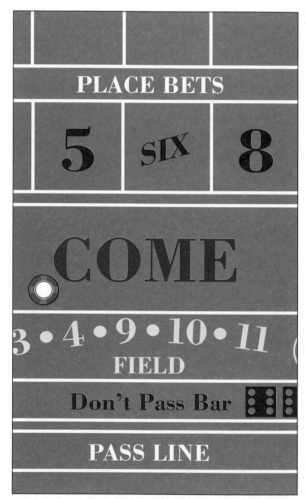

Come bets can be made anytime after a point is established. That roll is essentially a come-out roll for that bet. If a seven is rolled the bet wins, but your pass line bet loses. If a point is established, the shooter must roll that number again before he rolls a seven.

seven or a four is rolled. The next roll is technically a come-out roll, but since this bet has to be resolved, it will remain in action.

● The shooter rolls a five, six, eight, nine or ten. The come line bet is moved to the corresponding place bet box, and becomes a separate bet that will only be resolved when a seven or that specific number is rolled. The pass line bet remains.

Just as with a pass line bet, you should take odds with a come line bet. When a point is established for your come bet, the dealer will move that chip to a position in the place bet box that corresponds to your position at the table.

You may not touch those chips, so to make an odds bet, you must announce to the dealer that you'd like odds on that bet. Since there is not much room in the place bet box, the dealer will place the odds bet on top of the come line bet, offset just a little to indicate that it is payable at true odds.

Let's place one more come bet. You already have action on the pass line (the point is four). Let's say the first come bet roll was a six, so your bet is moved to place bet box six. Six results could occur:

● The shooter rolls a four. You win your pass line bet (and accompanying odds). Your first come bet (six is the point) is still in action, and your second come bet is moved to place bet box four.
● The shooter rolls a seven. You lose both your pass line and first come bets (and accompanying odds), but you win your second come bet.
● The shooter rolls an 11. You win your second come bet, and the pass line and first come line bets remain.
● The shooter rolls a two, three or 12. You lose your second come bet, and the pass line and first come line bets remain.
● The shooter rolls a five, eight, nine or ten. The dealer moves your second come bet to the corresponding place bet box, and the pass line and first come line bets remain. You now have action on three separate numbers.
● The shooter rolls a six. The dealer pays you for your first come bet, along with the odds, and slides the chips to you. He then takes the second come bet and places it in place bet box six. You still have your pass line bet, and now have a come line bet on the six.

A couple of things to remember about come bets. Since the come line bets are just like the pass line, you may not remove them until they have been resolved. Once again, the

casino will allow you to take down your odds bets on come line bets at any time.

A PLACE IN THE SUN

Another way to bet multiple numbers at a craps game is to "place" your bets. These bets can be made at any time. To place a bet, following the come out roll, you simply tell the dealer you'd like to "place the six" or any of the other place numbers—four, five, six, eight, nine and ten—you'd like to take.

Unlike the come line bets, the dealer must take the chips from you and place the bets. In no situation should the player ever reach above the come line, which is the unofficial dividing point between the players and the dealers. He places the chips in a corresponding position to your playing position at the table, so he can easily identify which bets belong to which players.

The payoffs for the place numbers are as follows:
● For the four and ten, nine to five;

Place and buy bets can only be set up by the dealer. To make this bet, simply tell the dealer you want to 'place' a particular number. Place bets are not paid at true odds, while buy bets are because you pay a commission to 'buy' those bets.

● For the five and nine, seven to five;
● For the six and eight, seven to six.

Right now you're saying "Why should I place on the four or ten at a payoff of nine to five, when I can bet a come bet, place the odds and get two-to-one on the payoff?"

The answer is that on the come line, you've got to wait for the number to hit before you can take odds. And you'll get no payoff if you bet the come; your bet will simply be moved to the place bet box number. Then you have to wait for the number to hit a second time before you get a payoff.

If you place a number, you get paid the first time it hits. But you pay a big edge by placing your number bets. The casino advantage for the four and ten is a large 6.7 percent. For the five and nine, the edge is four percent, and for the six and eight, it's a more reasonable 1.5 percent.

It is only advisable to take the six and eight because of the small edge, as well as the six and eight are the second most likely combinations to be rolled outside of the seven.

If you do bet these numbers, you must make the exact bets, or you won't get a full payoff. For instance, you must bet $6 to win $7 on the six and eight. For the five and nine, $5 will get you $7, and for the four and ten, $5 will win $9. If you're betting higher, bet in multiples of those amounts. Anything less, and the house will further expand its advantage.

Place bets can be taken down at any time. Simply ask the dealer to "Take me down" and you'll get all your bets back. Place bets are also "off" or "not working" on the come out roll.

BUYING THE LUCK

Another way of getting the true odds is to "buy" the numbers. When you buy the numbers, the house charges a five percent commission. But since most casinos only deal with $1 chips as the lowest denomination, and the house will charge you a minimum of $1 no matter how small your bet is, you should be betting at least $20 on each number, since $1 is five percent of $20. So if you want to buy the five, for example, you'd give the dealer $21. The dealer will place $20 on the number, and put $1 into the bank.

The rationale for buying numbers is that you get the true payoff, which lowers the house advantage, but not sufficiently to make it a good bet. The true odds payoffs are as follows:
● For the four and ten, two to one;
● For the five and nine, three to two;
● For the six and eight, six to five.

Because you pay the one percent commission, or "vig" and get paid at the true odds, the house has the same edge for all the numbers, 4.76 percent.

So you can see, it's more advantageous to place the six and eight, and the five and nine, because the house edge for those bets when they are placed, is less than the buy option. Only the four and ten is a better "buy" if you'll excuse the expression.

The dealer places a small plastic "buy" disk on top of any buy bet to indicate how the bet should be paid.

DOING THE DON'TS

Most craps players like to bet the pass line. But there's another bet at the table that offers the same edge, but is shunned by the vast majority. It is a bet on the don't pass line, sometimes called the "wrong" bettor. Some long-time observers of the game say only one in ten craps players bets the don't pass line and the other bets that go along with it, despite the fact that it offers the same low 1.4 percent house edge as the pass line.

Why is that? The don't pass line can be one of the most exciting bets, and after the come out roll, the edge is clearly in favor of the don't better.

There are a couple of major reasons why the don't pass bettor is a rare bird in the casino. The main reason is that if you're betting the don't, you're betting against the shooter.

While this obviously doesn't affect how he rolls the dice, it nonetheless is taken as an affront. It takes a special kind of person to stand up to the disdain of the shooter, and the players who are betting with them.

Players who bet the don't are often accused of betting "with" the house by other bettors. This is obviously ridiculous. The casino pays off both bets, and if everyone at the table were betting the don't, the casino would have to pay off the entire table just the same as if they're betting the "do". Because most players bet the "do" however, players assume that the house must be rooting for the don't, hence the mistaken idea that don't bettors are allied with the casino.

The second reason people rarely bet the don't is that it is a grind. You rarely make the big score by betting the don't. You are playing in hope of a choppy table—a pass, a miss, a miss, a pass, and a few more misses. A pass player is looking for the hot streak—a long string of passes—while the don't player will only win when the shooter rolls a consistent number of sevens.

It's not difficult to understand the don't pass line. It's the exact opposite of the pass line. All the rules are reversed. The don't bettor:
● Loses if the come-out roll is seven or 11;
● Wins if two or three is thrown on the come-out roll;

● Since the 12 is "barred" on the come-out roll, the wrong bettor pushes. There is no decision either way for the don't bettor;
● If a number is rolled on the come-out roll—four, five, six, eight, nine or ten, the don't bettor will win if the shooter rolls a seven before that number repeats;

The key is the seven on the come out roll. If a point is established the odds are clearly in favor of the don't bettor. After a point is established, the don't better has twice as many chances to win than a four or a ten. The don't bettor will win three times to every two for the five and the nine, and six times for every five for the six and the eight. It won't surprise you then to understand why the casino will let you take down your don't bet when it insists that pass line bets remain in action until it is resolved. When you have the edge, the casino would love to get off the hook.

ODDS: DO OR DON'T

While you take odds on the pass line, you lay odds on the don't pass line. It costs more money to win less, however, because, once again, the odds are the reverse of the pass line.

Let's say the point is four. The "right" bettor takes odds of two-to-one since he has six ways of losing, while only three ways of winning. If the single-odds bet is $5, and a four is rolled, the right bettor will win $10. The wrong bettor makes the opposite wager. He must bet $10 to win $5 if the seven appears before the four.

The same is true for the other numbers. For a five or nine, a $5 don't bet, a player must bet $9 to win $6. For the six or eight, the don't bettor lays $6 to win $5.

Unlike the pass line, where you place your odds bet behind the pass line, the odds bet is either heeled (offset on top of your original bet) or "bridged" (two chips of equal value with a third, or more, chips on top, or bridged, across them both). And again, because the house has no advantage on these odds, they can be removed at any time.

THE DON'T COME

Once again, the don't come bet is the opposite of the come. It is made after a point is established and is independent of

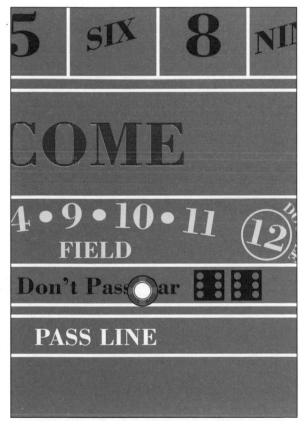

A gambler who makes a don't pass bet is often referred to as a 'wrong' bettor. He sometimes incurs the wrath of his fellow gamblers for betting against them.

DON'T BET	HOUSE EDGE
No odds	1.41%
Single odds	0.83%
Double odds	0.59%
Triple odds	0.46%
5 x odds	0.32%
10 x odds	0.18%

A don't come bettor is doing exactly the opposite of the come bettor. After a point is established, he clearly has the advantage.

the don't pass bets. The same rules apply to the don't come bet as to the don't pass bet on the come-out roll. If a point number is rolled, the dealer moves the bet to an area above the place bet boxes, and this bet wins if a seven is rolled before the point number is repeated. You may lay odds on the don't come bets the same way you do on come bets. The amount and ration of the odds bets are the same as those of the odds on a don't pass bet.

THE ODDS CONTROVERSY

Some experts say that by taking odds on your don't come bet, you dilute your advantage after the point has been established. That is not true, because even though you have

to put up more money to win less, you are reducing the house edge each time you multiply the odds bet.

Take a look at how much a don't pass bet with odds cuts the house advantage:

THE REAL DON'TS OF CRAPS

As you see, many of the best bets in the casino are found at the craps table. The pass and don't pass lines, come and don't come, some of the place bets and, most effectively, taking odds on the pass or don't pass bets, offer some of the smallest risks you'll find at any casino game.

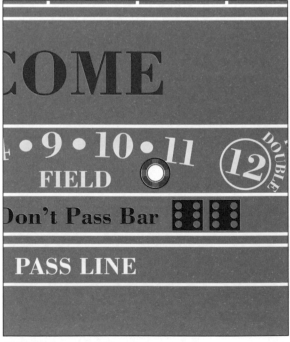

Field bets.

Conversely, however, many of the worst bets in the house are also emblazoned across the craps layout. In most cases, the worst bets will give the player the largest betting area. The stickman will act like a huckster, and try to sell these long-shot wagers. Only an intelligent player will be able to understand why it's important to avoid those bets. Since most of the bets are resolved by one roll of the dice, it's easy to estimate their handicap. There are good reasons for them being known as "sucker" bets.

PROP BETS

The bulk of the bad bets at the craps table are "proposition bets". They can be exciting because they offer a big payday, but the actual payoff does not reflect the true odds. They are heavily advertised on the craps layout, via a large box in front of the stickman.

Whenever one of these bets hits, a good stickman will invariably make a big stir about the payoff, trying to entice bets from other less knowledgeable craps players.

The payoffs on these bets range from four-to-one to 30-to-one, but the house edge runs from 9.1 percent to 16.7 percent. In most cases, players can get better odds on nickel slot machines.

The worst bet at the dice table is one that sounds rather plausible, so inexperienced players are tempted to place it. By making the "any seven" bet, these players are hoping that the shooter will roll a seven on the next roll. It seems reasonable since there are more ways to make a seven (six ways), than any other number. But the payoff does not reflect the many other numbers that can be rolled, so the any seven bet carries a hefty 16.7 percent house edge. The true odds on any seven are five-to-one, but it only pays four-to-one.

Wagers on the two and twelve, or the three and the eleven are to be avoided as well. The bet for the two and twelve is marginally worse than the three or eleven, giving the house a 13.9 percent advantage. The true odds are 35-to-one, but the casino only pays 30-to-one. That costs the $5 bettor $25, even though the craps initiate would be thrilled with a $150 win.

True odds on the three and eleven prop bet is 17-to-one, but the house only pays 15-to-one, gaining an 11.1 percent edge.

The "any craps" bet seems like fun. After all, it's the name of the game, and the two, three and twelve are house numbers on the come out roll because it beats all the pass line bettors. But the odds are prohibitive. Any craps bettors are giving the house a 11.11 percent edge.

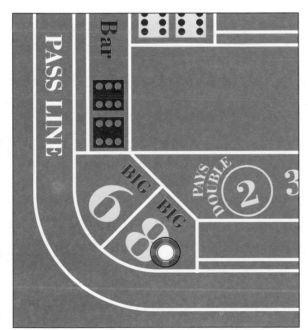

Big 6 & 8.

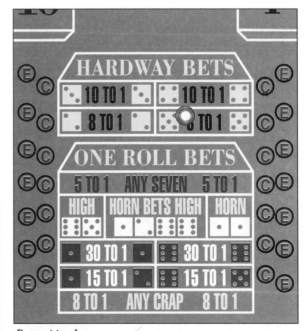

Proposition bets.

Some pass line bettors make the any craps bets to take "insurance" on their come out bets. For instance, if a player makes a $15 bet on the pass line, he may make a $2 any craps bet. If a two, three or twelve is rolled, he loses the pass line bet, but gets paid seven-to-one, or $14 for his any craps bet, reducing his net loss to $1.

Resist this reasoning, however. Each bet is independent of the other, and making the two bets does nothing to reduce the house edge. It merely exposes more of the player's money, hastening his downfall.

Hardways bets are another tempting wager, especially if the point, established on the come-out roll, is one of these numbers. By making a number the "hardway", the player rolls a pair of any number. A hard six (two threes) or hard eight (two fours) pays nine-to-one, but carries a house edge of 9.1 percent. The hard four or ten pays seven-to-one, giving away 11.11 percent. Betting the hardways is a hard way to win.

BIG FIELD BETS

One of the most popular bets for inexperienced craps players is the field bet. Once again, it seems like a good bet. The betting area occupies a large chunk of the craps layout at each end of the table. For the table minimum, a player can wager that the two, three, four, nine, ten, eleven or twelve will appear on the next roll. Only a five, six, seven or eight will defeat that bet. The bet pays even money.

But take a closer look. Even though the field numbers winners seem to be more numerous than the losers, it's simply not true. The amount of dice combinations that make up those seven numbers totals 16. But there are 20 ways to roll the five, six, seven and eight, so the player is giving the house a 5.56 percent advantage. Looks can be deceiving in craps.

Another well advertised bet at most dice games (except in Atlantic City) is the big six or eight. Because the six and eight are rolled so frequently, players mistakenly believe it is a good bet. By placing this bet, the player is wagering that a six or eight will appear before a seven is rolled.

It is the same bet as a place bet on the six or eight, but the payoff is considerably worse. By placing the six or eight, the player receives a seven-to-six payoff, but a winning wager

on the big six or eight only gets even money. A casino advantage of 9.09 percent means the player will lose $1 for every $11 wagered. By placing the six or eight, players are dramatically reducing the casino's edge to only 1.5 percent, meaning a player loses $1 for every $66 bet. But you won't see that advertised anywhere. Only the most knowledgeable players realize they can get the best bets at the craps tables, while avoiding the "sucker" bets.

DICE BETS TO AVOID

BET	PAYOFF	HOUSE EDGE
Any Seven	4-1	16.7%
Two	30-1	13.9%
Twelve	30-1	13.9%
Three	15-1	11.1%
Eleven	15-1	11.1%
Any Craps	7-1	11.1%
Hard Six	9-1	9.1%
Hard Eight	9-1	9.1%
Hard Four	7-1	11.1%
Hard Ten	7-1	11.1%
Field	1-1	5.6%
Big Six, Eight	1-1	9.1%

THE LANGUAGE
OF DICE

Casinos have their own language, like any specialized occupation or sideline, but no game has a more colorful shouting slang than craps. Much of this heritage has been lost as the legendary craps players head for the big game in the sky, but novice players would do well to review expressions they just might hear while playing their initial dice games.

The language of craps may be divided into two categories: colorful expressions craps shooters say to encourage the dice to roll their way, and the phrases dealers and stickmen use to accept a bet or announce a roll of the dice.

The point numbers have all been given names, and with the exception of the Five and Ten, all have home towns that rhyme with their names.

The four is often called Little Joe from Kokomo, while the five is sometimes known as Little Phoebe. She has no hometown, but her cousin, Fiver, Fiver, Racetrack Driver, at least has a job. Our best friends, the six and eight are Southerners, known as Sixie from Dixie and Eighter from Decatur. Perhaps the nine was named after a former Rose Bowl Queen, Nina from Pasadena.

The Ten usually goes by the name of Big Dick, but his hardway cousin, the five-five, is sometimes referred to as Hard Ten, Ladies' Best Friend.

The dots on the dice have spawned a variety of other names. Snake's Eyes is a pair of aces. Old-timers refer to the ace-deuce as Cross-Eyes, while Chopsticks and Rabbit Tracks are favored nicknames for the hard six. Windows or the Square Pair is the hard eight. Twelves are usually known as Boxcars, but on occasion are called Sergeant's Stripes, a reflection of the barracks games where many players cut their craps teeth.The bets you can make have some distinctive names. The Buffalo Bet, for example, means that you put $1 each on all the hardways and $1 on the "any seven". A bet you'll still hear a lot at the table is "C and E" which means "any craps" and "eleven". On the odd rare occasion, you will hear this called "Chester and Esther".

Probably the most common word in craps today is "Yo!", meaning Eleven. Legend has it that some long-forgotten dealer pronounced his elevens "yo-leven." If you want to use it at the craps table, be sure to shout it with feeling.

THE SYSTEMS APPROACH

WHEN WRONG IS RIGHT

You wouldn't notice Jack at a craps table. He's not like many craps players, who get excited every time they win a bet. Jack tries to wedge himself in next to the dealer and keep a low profile. You see, Jack is something of a pariah at the dice game. Even though he's quiet and reserved, as well as being a true gentleman, Jack might as well be the devil himself. You see, Jack is a wrong bettor.

There's nothing that will aggravate a volatile shooter more than someone who consistently bets against him. He might not say anything for a while, but it eats at him. And finally it will explode, especially if the wrong bettor wins more than the shooter.

Jack wins fairly consistently, making it all the worse. He's got a simple system, and has refined it over the years to recognize those "cold" craps games that are so valued by wrong bettors.

Just as the don't player bets completely the opposite from the right player, Jack is attracted to completely the opposite type of game. After scouting the casino for the quietest craps table, one where the players seem to be just pushing their chips from the pass line to the table chip bank, he slides into position to begin playing.

He buys in for $250, and waits for a come-out roll. He places a $5 bet on the don't pass line, and when a point is established, he'll add single odds. He'll make two don't come bets, and add single odds to those wagers. If he wins those bets, he'll begin over again with the same $5 don't pass bet, but add double odds when a point is established. Two more don't come bets, with double odds on those bets, and he'll wait for a resolution.

If he wins, the $5 don't pass bet will be topped by triple odds, and two don't come bets will complete his wagers.

If he loses, it's back to square one, and the single odds. When Jack reaches the odds limit, he'll double his initial wager until he loses.

With this system, Jack wins more than he loses and keeps his losses to a minimum. If a player makes three passes, he stops betting until the "hot" streak passes.

No, Jack doesn't win a fortune with his system, but then again, he never blows his entire bankroll, like the shooter at the other end of the table who is waiting for his "dream" roll, and cursing Jack all the way.

CHAPTER 7

POKER

KNOW WHEN TO HOLD 'EM

The most famous game in the casino is poker and it gives skillful players the best chance to make money, but you don't have to wear a stetson and drink whiskey to learn the ropes.

Of all the casino games, there is none as familiar to the public as poker. Although its roots are said to spring from European card games of the middle ages, poker could be described as the one truly all-American game. Since the 1850s, poker has been a staple in any gambling hall, legal or illegal. More Americans have played poker than have played golf, tennis and backgammon combined.

Whether they learned around the kitchen table, with a wise aunt or uncle showing them the ropes, or got involved in a hot game in the boys' room in grammar school, most poker players can trace their joy of the game back to childhood. And whether they play for big stakes, nickels and dimes, or for matchsticks, the players' enjoyment of poker is the reason it is undoubtedly the most popular card game.

Even when casino gambling was legal only in Nevada, poker could regularly be found in fire halls, social clubs, church basements, and fraternal organizations. It is now played legally in more than half the United States, and semi-legally in all the other states and territories.

As you might suspect casino poker varies a bit from your kitchen table variety, but the basics are essentially the same. What is most different in the casino is the skill levels of the players.

You might be the card shark of your neighborhood, but when you play poker in a casino, there are many other factors to consider, other than which player has the best hand.

You've seen that there are professional blackjack players who can make a living playing a game in which they can reduce or eliminate the house edge. And you learned that good sports bettors can handicap a sporting event through knowledge of specific details unknown to the average better. But since poker is a game that has no house edge, you must be prepared for a large collection of players who are trying to make a living from poker. There are more professional poker players than any other type of gambler.

Don't be fooled into thinking that all the "professionals" are playing the high limit games, and if you play games with $1 minimum and $4 maximum bets, you won't have to worry about the pros. That's not true. You'll meet the professional poker players at every level, whether they are on the way up the ladder, or have been knocked down and are looking to get back up.

Should this deter you from playing America's most popular game in a casino? The answer is a qualified "no".

Because poker requires skill, it's not something where you

POKER GOALS

can hope to stumble across enough good luck to win. While there is some debate on how skill is acquired (are good poker players born or made?) you can read enough about the game to understand its nuances and sit down and enjoy a lively session. Just remember that you never stop learning about poker. After getting the basics down, your education is just beginning. The various plays, the different combinations, but most of all, the variety of players is what often makes this game the most fascinating game of all.

There are many different kinds of poker games. Five-card draw and five-card stud may be popular around the kitchen table, but are now a rarity in the casinos. Forget about the "wild card" games they play down at the fire hall. You won't see any Deuces wild, one-eyed Jacks, or Jokers added to a poker game in a casino. The two most popular poker games by far in a casino are seven-card stud and Texas hold'em.

While there are many other poker permutations that you can find—Omaha hold'em, Omaha Eight-or-better, razz, lowball draw and many more—for purposes of brevity and comprehension, you'll be wise to concentrate on the two most popular games, which will be covered in this book.

The obvious object of poker is to win the pot. That is easier said than done, but there are two ways to accomplish that goal. The first is to have the best hand at the table, and the second is to convince the other players that you have the best hand so they'll drop out and leave you the pot. This is called bluffing, and is not nearly as successful as many of the experts would have you believe.

Before you begin to play, the most important thing to understand is the ranking of hands in poker. Many a game has been lost when a player—usually a beginner, but sometimes an experienced player—forgets which hand beats which. The most frequently confused hands are the full house, flush and straight. Commit to memory the chart in this chapter before even considering venturing out into the cruel world of casino poker.

Most poker games, including seven-card stud and Texas hold'em, use this ranking, which are the best hands, using five cards.

ROYAL FLUSH

FOUR OF A KIND

STRAIGHT FLUSH

FULL HOUSE

FLUSH

THREE OF A KIND

STRAIGHT

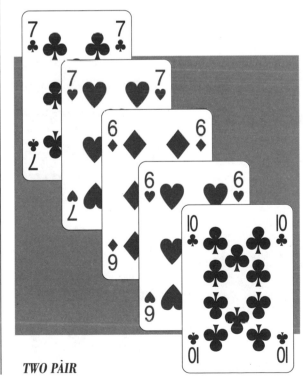

TWO PAIR

PAIR

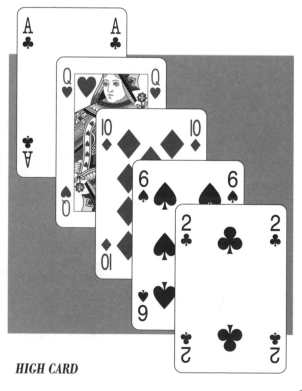

HIGH CARD

POKER PROCEDURES

It's also important to realize that casino rules are vastly different from those that you employ in a friendly family game. If these rules are ignored or violated it may cost you a very valuable pot.

The chief advantage to playing in a casino is that the house provides a dealer. You don't have to worry about Uncle Joe dealing from the bottom of the deck or some card shark dealing "second", saving the best card on top for himself and dealing the cards underneath to the other players.

It will cost you a little to play in a casino. Because there is no casino advantage in poker, the house charges players for providing the space and the personnel to offer an honest game. In most casinos, the house will take a "rake" from each pot. A rake is a percentage of the pot that is taken out by the dealer after every round of betting. This percentage will vary between five and ten percent, and most casinos put a limit on how much money will be withdrawn from each pot.

In some other jurisdictions, the house charges a "seat rental". This is usually an hourly fee that progresses upward with the limits.

Unlike poker played at home, casino poker doesn't necessarily require an "ante" or bet prior to receiving the initial cards. In Texas hold'em, a "blind" is used. A blind is when one or sometimes two players put up a small ante before a round begins. The blind is rotated in clockwise direction around the table.

When betting commences, you must bet in a prescribed sequence depending upon the rules of the specific game. The person with the high hand will make a bet in seven-card stud. The player to his left then must "call" (match that bet), "raise" (increase the bet), or "fold" (throw his cards in and withdraw from the hand). A player who acts out of turn can influence the play of the others, so it is important to take your cue from the dealer as to the correct time to make your bet.

In Texas hold'em, the first "live" player to the left of the "dealer" makes the initial wager. A live player is one who has not folded on a previous round. And while the casino uses a dealer at Texas hold'em, each round, a player is designated as the "dealer" so that the deal will start with a different player to the immediate left of that designated dealer on each round. The "dealer" is indicated by a "button" in hold'em.

It's important never to throw your chips into the pot. The dealer must make certain that each bet contains the correct amount of money, and throwing the money into the pot will require him to root through the pot to find your chips, dramatically slowing down the game. When you bet, simply place your chips in front of you. After the round of betting is complete, the dealer will reach out and sweep all the chips into the middle of the pot. When you are going to raise, tell the dealer. Don't put a partial bet out and return to your chips to complete the bet. Be prepared to make your bet when it's your turn. No one likes a player who slows down the game. Do your thinking when other players are acting. Although you are permitted to lift your hole cards off the table, the casino insists that you keep your cards over the table. Don't pull them down into your lap to get a better look. The dealer is responsible for all the cards, and must be sure that your are not trying to sneak in different cards.

Maybe the hardest rule to understand in casinos is what is known as "table stakes". This rule limits you to betting the chips in front of you. If you run out of chips, you cannot go back into your pocket for more money to call or raise.

This has implications for those who approach poker with a money management system. Let's say that you have a $100 loss limit. You've entered a seven-card poker game with a $1 minimum and $4 maximum bet. Luck is running against you, and you've reduced your stake to only about $20. Instead of buying in to raise your table stakes to an acceptable level, you decide to keep playing and hope to get moderately lucky to build your bankroll back up. Unfortunately, this is usually the time you get struck by lightning. You draw four-of-a-kind in the first five cards, and other players at the table have decent hands, as well. Everyone is raising and calling, but before long, you're out of money.

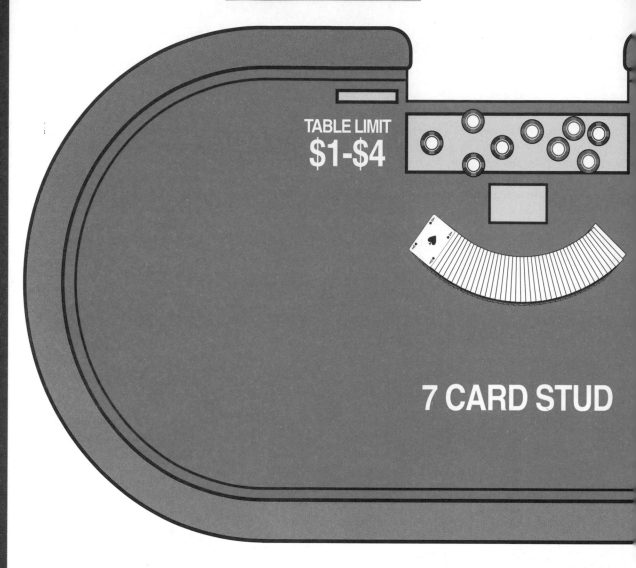

TABLE LIMIT $1-$4

7 CARD STUD

At this point, you have to call "all in". The dealer than separates all future bets from the pot which contains your money. The betting continues furiously and you can only watch. Now, you're not out of the game. You continue to receive cards and have a stake in the pot that contains your bets, but all the bets being made as you watch will be awarded to someone else. Sure, you're going to win the original pot, because the odds that someone will beat your four-of-a-kind are remote, at best.

The money in the side pot will go to the remaining player with the second-best hand.

While you can still approach poker with a money management attitude, you must be prepared to get lucky and to back it up with chips as ammunition.

While there is no "rule" or "procedure", it is considered rude and tactless to talk about your hand, whether live or discarded, while the game is proceeding. When the time comes to show your hand, turn up all your cards, not just the five cards that make up the hand. You may be missing a better hand, and the other players have a right to see the two cards you are not using to make your hand. If no one calls or raises your final bet, you do not have to show any of your cards, and no experienced player will ask to see them.

And finally, to show your appreciation for the job done by the dealer, you should tip him or her whenever you win an average-sized pot. This is not obligatory, but it's considered

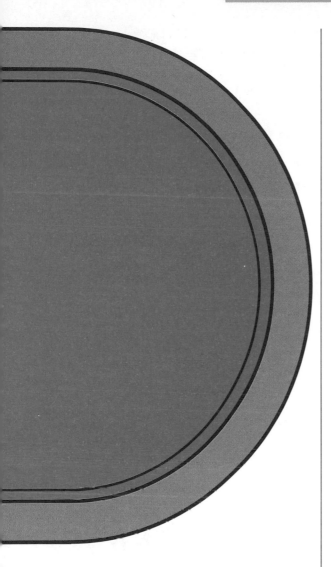

known as "third street". The second is whether to continue to bet when the fifth card is dealt, a point in the game known as "fifth street". This is undoubtedly the last point you can exit the game profitably by throwing in your hand.

It's true that every decision you make at seven-card stud can be important, and any mistake can prove costly, but by mastering the possibilities at these two crucial points in the game, you have a much better chance to come out ahead at the end of the night.

STARTING SEVEN CARDS

While most low-limit seven-card stud games require no ante, the higher limit games frequently demand a modest ante. Before beginning play, ask the dealer about any procedures that may be unclear to you and he'll be glad to explain the play of that particular table.

As play begins, each player is dealt two cards face down and one upcard. The lowest card will be required to open the betting, with a bet known as the "bring-in". This player has no option, he's required to make at least the minimum bet. If two players have the identical low card, the alphabetical order of the suits—clubs, diamonds, hearts, spades—determines who opens the betting.

The player immediately to the left of the bring-in, now has the option to call the bet, to raise or to fold. If he folds or calls, the person immediately to his left has the same options. But if he raises, every player to his left must match that raise, raise further or fold. The game proceeds clockwise until every player has made his choice of how to act on that hand.

Each player receives three more cards face up, and the final card face down. There is a round of betting between each card, and in these subsequent deals, the player with the high hand has the responsibility to act first. If two hands are of equal value, the first player to the left of the dealer acts first. The betting session following the final card is known as the "river".

At this point, the player with the high hand is not required to bet. He can "check", which means that he's not going to bet, but pass the option to bet on to the next player. If another player makes a bet, the players remaining in the hand must at least match the bet.

A word about bets. For low-limit games, $1-$4 for example,

a time-honored poker tradition.

SEVEN-CARD STUD

One of the most complicated, but rewarding, of all poker games is seven-card stud. The sheer number of possible hands and permutations of combinations of cards makes it difficult to figure all the angles. But, then again, that's what makes it so interesting.

After you decide on the limit of the game you want to play, there are two crucial decisions to make early in the game. The first is whether to make an initial bet after the third card is dealt, or the to enter the first round of betting at the point the first player must bring in for $1, and initial bets are also for $1. Raises, on the other hand, may be from anywhere between $1 and $4.

Some games have double limits. For instance on a $3-$6 game, the bring in will be for $1, and all players must match that $1. If a raise is made, it must be for $3, at which point, all subsequent bets must be for $3, and raises must be in increments of $3. All bets and raises in the last two betting rounds must be in increments of $6. Once again, if this is confusing while you're playing the game, the dealer will be most helpful in explaining the betting procedures.

STRATEGY FOR SEVEN-CARD STUD

In seven-card stud, it costs nothing or very little to see your first three cards. It's important to be able to evaluate the value of those hands to decide whether you want to play them.

For instance, let's say you get three cards of the same suit.

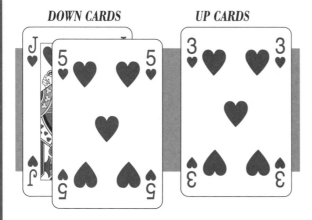

DOWN CARDS   *UP CARDS*

The correct play here would be to begin to bet, and hope that within the next four cards you receive, at least two will be in the hearts suit. But if you look around the table, and see three or more hearts already revealed, it's best to fold. Chances are, you're not going to make that flush.

You have to understand how the number of players affect the cards you are holding. For instance if you have a high pair like:

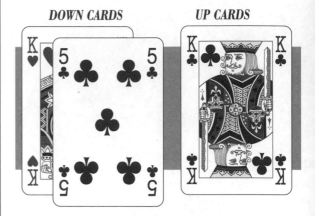

DOWN CARDS   *UP CARDS*

You are better off playing against just a couple of players. High pairs usually fare better when only a few players are competing, and you'll have the best chance of winning. But if you have a hand like:

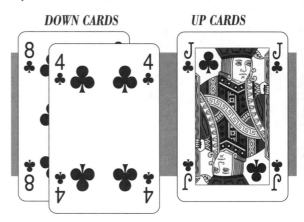

DOWN CARDS   *UP CARDS*

You'll want plenty of players in the game. When you have a high hand, you've got yours and the others have theirs to get.

When you have a drawing hand, or one that requires improvement, you will rarely make the hand, so that when you do, you want other players around to build up the pot you will win.

On the other hand, small or middle pairs are the most dangerous. Hands like:

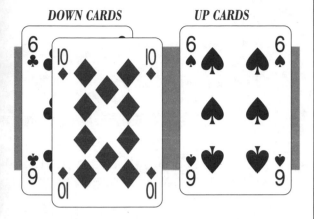

DOWN CARDS UP CARDS

Can cost you money because you're tempted to stay in hopes of getting a matching card or being able to "steal" the pot, win it with a mediocre hand after everyone else drops out. But while you're waiting to improve or get lucky, your opponent can easily match a higher pair that will make your pair look puny in comparison.

The opposite is true, as well. When you have high cards in your hand, and it appears that the most any opponent can have is a middle or low pair, you are in a good position to improve your hand. In a hand like:

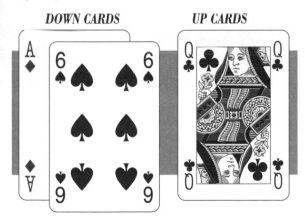

DOWN CARDS UP CARDS

You're in a good position to improve your hand by catching either another Ace or Queen.

Given the importance of the decisions made on third and fifth streets, once you've decided to pursue a pot, it's frequently a good idea to see it through. Many hands aren't made until the last card. But you must be aware of the

possible combinations of your opponents' hands. If you're chasing that high pair, and an opponent is raising with a hand like:

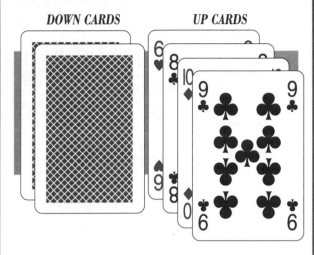

DOWN CARDS UP CARDS

You've got to assume that he's either made a straight, or wants you to think he's made a straight. A high pair won't be of much help in the first case, and it might cost you a good deal of money to prove the second case.

IT'S A START

As you can see, starting hands are crucial in seven-card stud, and unless you understand the value of starting hands, you'll be fleeced by the experienced players. In general, there are four categories of strength in starting hands.

1. Very Strong Hands: A hand that consists of three of the same cards is the poker player's dream. It won't happen often—only once in about 425 hands—but when it does, you've probably got a winner.

But you don't want to win just the antes and bring in bets, so you've got to be able to read the other players. Will a raise on the first round of betting chase out the other players? If you believe it will, you might want to hold off your first raise until at least the next round. On the other hand, if several players have already entered the pot, a raise is unlikely to force them to fold. Don't get too cocky, however. Three of a kind is a strong hand, but it does occasionally get beaten.

2. Strong Hands: A high pair is valuable in seven-card stud, but in most cases, it needs improvement. It is particularly dangerous if someone else has a higher pair. If this is the case, you should discard your hand, unless your kicker—your next highest card—is higher than your

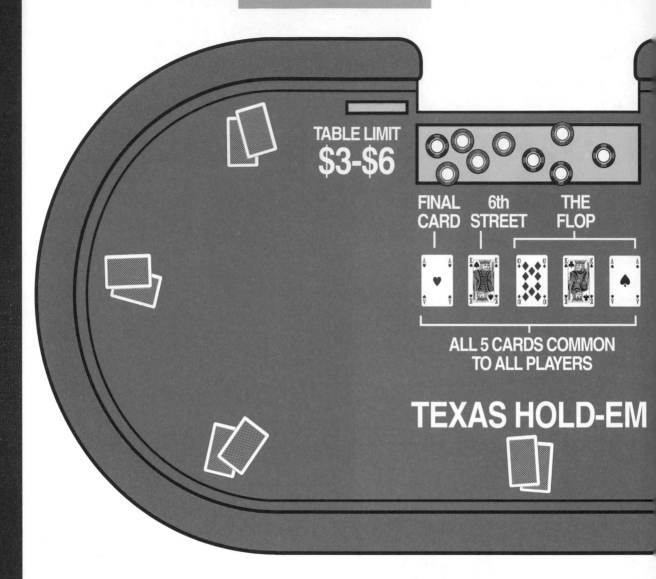

TABLE LIMIT
$3-$6

FINAL
CARD

6th
STREET

THE
FLOP

ALL 5 CARDS COMMON
TO ALL PLAYERS

TEXAS HOLD-EM

opponent's kicker. But this hand should be played aggressively, and in most cases, you'll play it to the river.

3. Good Hands: Whether and how to play small and middle pairs are sometimes the most complicated decision in seven-card stud. The most important factor is whether the cards you need to improve your hands are available. When you need another Four, for instance, and you see the third Four in your opponent's hand, it doesn't leave much of a chance to find the fourth in one of your draw cards. Another factor, however, is the size of your kicker. If you have a big card along with a small or medium pair, you've got another avenue to go if you get lucky.

4. Possible Hands: These are hands that need help, but

have the possibility to become good hands. They include three-card flushes and three-card straights. Once again, the upcards of your opponents will give you the best clue about how viable your hands are. And once again, the size of your kicker is a consideration in determining the value of this hand.

DOWN THE STREETS
As mentioned, all decisions made affect your ability to win. As the game proceeds, however, the decisions made can be very costly unless you understand the possibilities. You must be able to assess your opponents' cards and how they relate to your own hand.

Several strategies are called for in specific situations. If you

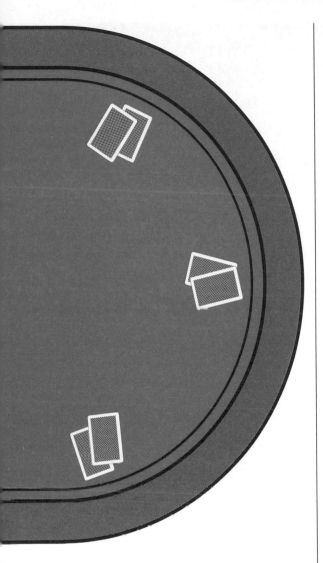

Another situation to beware of is when a player pairs an exposed card on the board. This gives him a good chance to have three of a kind. Even if he doesn't, he may have a quality hand. Unless you can beat him with a better hand, or you're looking at a particularly good pot, fold 'em.

Once you have decided to bet on fifth street, it rarely makes sense to fold before the river. The only exception to this rule is if you can clearly see that your hand cannot be improved enough on sixth street to beat a threatening hand held by an opponent. If you decide to go through on sixth street, do not fold on the river. If your opponent is bluffing, you have a chance to catch him at it, and you only have to expose a bluff once in a while to make it worth your while to go all the way.

STARTING ODDS

HAND	ODDS
Three-of-a-Kind	424-1
Pair of Aces	76-1
Three Suited Cards	18-1
Any Pair	5-1

TEXAS HOLD'EM

You wouldn't think that any game in which you only get two cards of your own would be very difficult or challenging, but until you've played Texas hold'em you can't imagine its permutations and complexity. To the uninitiated, hold'em looks like seven-card stud, with a few differences. In the end, however, the only thing that's the same is that the hands are made up of the best five of seven cards.

The critical differences begin with the starting hand. While this is always an important decision, it is not nearly as critical in hold'em as it is in seven-card stud. The decisions you make on the later streets make much more of a difference in your overall success in hold'em.

The most important difference between seven-card stud and Texas hold'em is the use of community cards, which are dealt face up in front of the dealer. These cards all play a part in the development of each player's hand.

STARTING HOLD'EM
Before any cards are dealt in Texas hold'em, the first player

make the hand you're looking for, bet it to the limit. If you pull a flush on sixth street, for instance, you should not check. Since some of your cards must be exposed, your opponent will suspect a flush, and not bet into your check. That means you'll lose a chance to get a double bet by every active player into the pot. If you check and give the active players a chance to get another card, there's a chance they may draw a hand that might beat your flush, costing you the entire pot. If you've got it, bet it.

If your opponent draws a third suited card, or a third card to a straight, only check or call. This is not a point to play aggressively, because if you raise, your opponent will undoubtedly raise, as well. It could end up costing you serious money.

to the left of the button must post a "small blind" which is a percentage of the minimum bet. The second player to the left of the button then posts a "big blind" which is usually equal to the table minimum. After posting these bets, the dealer distributes two cards to each player, beginning with the player who posted the small blind. Then the player to the left of the big blind has the option to fold, match the big blind, or raise. The betting then moves clockwise until all players have exercised their options. The players who posted the blinds have only to match the difference between the largest bet and the blinds to stay in the game. On subsequent betting rounds, the first active player to the left of the button initiates the betting.

After the first round of betting is completed, the dealer lays out three cards face up simultaneously in the middle of the table. This is called the "flop". Another round of betting takes place at that time. Betting also takes place between each of the next two face up cards, called fourth street and fifth street. Once again, these cards are all community cards that belong to all the active players.

When it's time for the showdown, the player with the best five cards using his two downcards and the five community cards is the winner. In Texas hold'em, there are frequently situations where players have the same hands. In this case, the pot is split.

Limits in Texas hold'em are similar to the situation mentioned in seven-card stud. The only difference would be the blinds. In a $3-$6 hold'em game, the first player would ante a small blind of $1, and the big blind would be $3.

HOLD'EM STRATEGY
Texas hold'em is an illusion. It appears to be a simple game, but you have to understand all the variables and how to make the correct play.

The most important, but probably most difficult aspect of hold'em, is to know what the best possible hand—known as "the nuts"—is, and whether any of your opponents could be holding it. For instance if the five community cards are:

COMMUNITY CARDS

There is no chance any player can be holding a straight, flush or full house. The best possible hand would be three Queens.

By assessing the number of players in the game, and their betting patterns, you'll get a hint about the best hand. The more players and the more raises in a game, the better the chance that one of the players has "the nuts".

It's important that you are able to recognize when you have the best possible hand. If you have the nuts and don't know it, you can lose out on a very profitable opportunity. But believing you have the nuts, and you really don't, can be much more costly to you.

For example, if you hold a hand such as:

And you have an Ace-King, you're a winner. You should get as much money into the pot and milk it for all it's worth. But if the Four of clubs is a Four of diamonds, you could lose to a flush.

In Texas hold'em, the betting position is more crucial than with any other poker game. That's because the game is a fixed-position game, rather than one where the lead-off bet has the high hand.

Since the players only see the community cards, it's not possible to discern who has the high hand in hold'em, so the betting proceeds from the player to the left of the button. Since it is always beneficial to act last in any poker game, you should be more selective of the hands you play when you bet from an early position, rather than when you are in a position near the end of the hand.

High cards are better than low cards. If you have two downcards like:

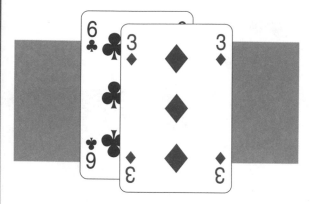

Throw them away. Even if you pair one or the other, there's very little chance no one else will come through with a higher pair.

Conversely, if your hand consists of:

You might want to consider seeing the flop. If you pair up one of those cards, you're in a much stronger position, particularly if the paired card is the highest of the flop.

Beware of suited cards. While they are valuable, having two in your hand is just that; it's only two toward a flush. It might end up costing you significant wagers chasing that fourth or fifth suited card.

GETTING DOWN TO BUSINESS

As mentioned earlier, starting hands are not as crucial as seven–card stud. But that's not to say they are not important. The following are five categories, ranked in order of importance, that are considered good starting hands and will give you an excellent chance to win the hold'em pot.

● **High Pairs:** When you have a pair of Tens or higher, you're in a good position. With a high pair, you have a chance to improve your hand, but even if you don't match any cards on the board, you can steal the hand because your opponents will have no idea why you're betting so strongly late in the hand.
A hand like:

Is strong, particularly if not one of the five community cards is higher than a Queen. But if you match the Queen, you're in the driver's seat.

● **Small Pairs:** As in most poker games, the difference between winning and losing is often the difference between small and large pairs.
A hand like:

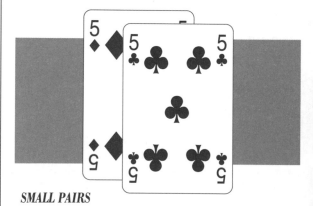

SMALL PAIRS

Will rarely win unless you're able to improve it in some way. The odds against improving a pair to three of a kind in hold'em is eight-to-one against. These hands should be classified as drawing hands, and must be played carefully.

● **Two High Cards:** While two high cards are a playable hand, it is not very valuable. A hand like an Ace-King should always be played, but a hand such as:

TWO HIGH CARDS

Should, in most cases, be folded, particularly if someone raises. If the two cards are suited, you definitely should play it, just be aware not to overrate the suited cards.

● **Suited Connectors:** Two cards that could lead to straights are called connectors, but two suited cards could also lead to a flush. Consider, for example, the following hand:

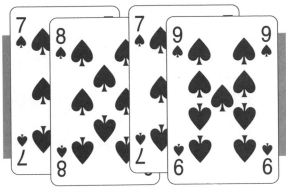

SUITED CONNECTORS

It's only a mediocre hand, but it has possibilities. If there is a gap between the cards: Seven of Spades, Nine of Spades It's worth even less. Fold it unless you're the blind and don't have to match any raises.

● **High-low suited:** If you have a high card along with a low card, and they're both suited, you have a basis for seeing the flop, as long as there aren't any serious raises. A hand like:

HIGH LOW SUITED

Wouldn't be very valuable if it wasn't for the suited aspect of the cards. But it is more valuable than a lower high card, a Queen of Diamonds, for instance. Play the Ace whenever it doesn't cost you much, particularly if you're the blind and don't have to match a raise.

All other hands should be folded. The chance of making something out of two totally unrelated cards isn't worth matching the blind and possibly meeting a raise. By carefully studying every situation, you will realize that only by getting the best chance to win with a favorable starting hand is worth playing.

AFTER THE FLOP
You've decided that your starting hand is strong enough to continue to play, and you've matched the blind and any raises to see the flop. You've entered the area which will determine how far you go; the crucial stage in Texas hold'em.

If you've entered the flop with two suited cards and the flop contains two more of your suited cards:

Hole cards   *Flop*

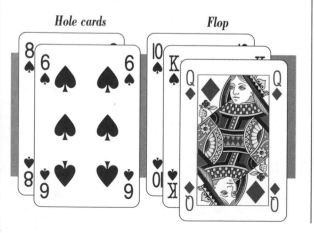

You should definitely bet. While your hand currently has no value, there are two reasons why you should bet as if it did. First, you may get that fifth card for the flush, which will give you an almost certain winner. Second, by betting, you may chase some or all of the other players out of the game, allowing you to steal the pot.

If you don't improve your hand on the flop, it's probably a good idea to fold and look ahead to the next hand. In most hold'em games, you'll encounter a raise on the betting round following the flop. If you're dealt something like:

Hole cards   *Flop*

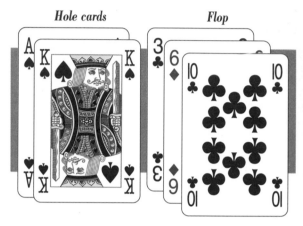

There's not a lot that can happen in subsequent rounds that will improve your hand sufficiently. And with two suited cards on board, you may be bucking a flush by an opponent.

Occasionally you'll have a great starting hand, such as a high pair, but the cards that fall from the flop do you no good. Even worse, they seem to have helped one of your opponents to a hand that will crush your pair:

Hole cards   *Flop*

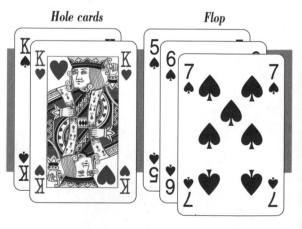

Unless you're willing to spend a lot of money to find out whether your opponent has a straight, a flush, or even worse, a straight flush, you have to bite the bullet and throw away your pair.

Like high pairs that face a completely different situation on the flop that may aid an opponent, low pairs that aren't helped by the flop should usually be folded. For instance, if you hold:

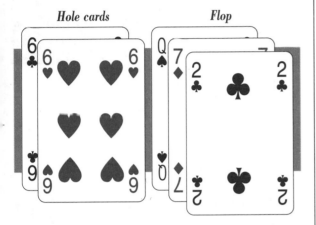

Hole cards   *Flop*

It's going to cost you substantial bets and raises to see the last two cards, and the chances are that you're not going to match those Sixes. Save your money and get out gracefully.

When you're drawing for a flush, and a pair shows on the flop, you should continue to play, even though you may be eventually beaten by a full house:

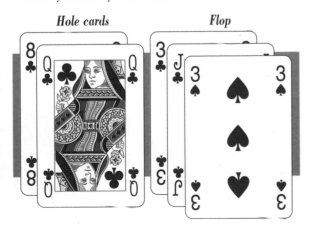

Hole cards   *Flop*

If your opponent has a three in the hole, or another pair, he simply has to match one more card to obtain his full house. But because you're only facing two-to-one odds, although you'll lose to a full house, the risk is worth it.

Sometimes, you may get what you're hoping for, but by observing the betting of other players, you have to conclude that what you have probably isn't enough to win. For instance, if you hold:

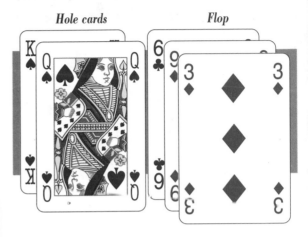

Hole cards   *Flop*

You're working on a flush, which in most cases is a valuable hand. But if someone is holding a Five-Nine in the hole, there's a good chance you'll get beat. Or even worse, a Nine-Ten will be almost unbeatable.

PLAYING ATTENTION

Because Texas hold'em uses the five community cards, there are many combinations of cards possible, creating many different hands. That's why it's very important to pay attention to the community cards and the action taken by all the players to be able to discern exactly what hand your opponents are pursuing or what hands they actually have.

The following hand will demonstrate how the game plays and the possible results of each hand. This is a perfect illustration of how you must be aware of all the potential hands created by the community cards and the players' individual hole cards.

In Texas hold'em, it is important to understand the relationship between the cards on the table and the cards in your hand. It is rare to hold a hand that couldn't be beaten by someone else playing that hand. Sometimes when it appears you can be beaten you may be holding a card that can block your opponents hands. Maintaining your composure and examining every possible outcome of a particular hand is crucial to success in hold'em.

Community Cards:

COMMUNITY CARDS

Player One: (You):

PLAYER ONE (YOU)

Player Two: King of Diamonds, Six of Hearts

PLAYER TWO

Player Three: Nine of Hearts, Nine of Spades

PLAYER THREE

Player Four: Eight of Hearts, Seven of Clubs

PLAYER FOUR

Player Five: Two of Spades, Ten of Spades

PLAYER FIVE

You think you've got a winner because you've got the top pair. You've been betting heavily all along, and can't understand why you haven't chased any of the other players out of the game. Here's why. Player Two beats you with two pair. Player Three beats you and Player Two with three-of-a-kind—"trips". Player Four has a straight, and which beats Player Three's trips, Player Two's two pair, and your high pair. But Player Five takes the pot. His flush beats everyone at the table. This has got to be a great pot!

THE SYSTEMS APPROACH

THE POKER PRO

Michael quit his regular job several years ago for a new profession. He now plays poker for a living, and does very well, thank you.

Michael didn't turn into a poker player overnight. It took years of playing poker as a hobby before he took the plunge. And now that he frequents the poker rooms of Las Vegas on a daily basis, he understands that he must play with a discipline he could only imagine when he was playing for recreation. That's why he follows six simple principles.

● Luck is often as important as skill: while professional poker players make their mortgage payment by utilizing the skill they have learned or otherwise acquired over the years, Michael understands that in the short term, anybody can get lucky. But, because of his experience, Michael is prepared to recognize that luck and take the greatest advantage of it. He is also realistic and understands that he will lose an occasional good hand to a "lucky" player. But just because he sees bad players get lucky, Michael knows it is important to always play his best. That way, luck can find you. You don't have to go looking for luck.

● When he does lose those good hands, Michael doesn't let it get to him, because he understands that he can only win consistently if he maintains a positive attitude. He sees players get discouraged all the time, and he knows that he has the advantage at that time, because a player with a negative attitude is more likely to play bad hands and make bad decisions.

● When he's playing, Michael sees his opponents stopping the cocktail waitress every time she goes by, to order a beer, mixed drink or some other alcoholic concoction. Michael used to drink in moderation when he played for entertainment, but now that he's a pro, he sticks with an occasional coffee. He also gets his rest every night (or day, depending upon when he decides to play), because he knows that playing when you're tired can cloud your reasoning and create mistakes.

● Because he depends upon his winnings for his living, Michael is cautious about betting more than he can afford. But that's nothing new. Michael knows that players who bet the rent money are nervous and on edge, a loser waiting to happen. It's a tired adage, but remains true nonetheless: never bet more than you can afford to lose.

● As a professional, Michael knows all the tricks. One he doesn't like to use, but often can't avoid is when a player shows his cards. Sure, it's inadvertent, but poker players are looking for every edge, and a player who is careless with his cards deserves to lose. Keeping your cards secure is one of the fundamental elements of playing winning poker.

● Most of all, Michael quit his regular job because he enjoys playing poker. If you're not having fun, it becomes just another job. The same holds true for playing for entertainment. If it becomes a chore, there's no reason to continue playing, it is supposed to be fun after all.

CHAPTER 8

SLOTS

THOSE SENSATIONAL SLOTS

When you get to betting on the slots you can, with a some luck, be talking about life-changing sums of money, but exactly how much luck do you need. It's man against machine, but does man really have a chance?

Many years ago, casino executives were surprised to discover that the money they were making at the table games was beginning to decline, and the profits generated by the slot machines were growing.

After all, to casino executives slot machines were really just a few toys they kept around to entertain the wives of the high rollers while their husbands were busy at the tables. It didn't make any sense that humble slot machines should be supplanting table game revenue.

But the casino executives just weren't paying attention. With computers becoming a vital part of every day life, young people developing an attraction to video games, and instant gratification turning the modern world upside-down, it was only natural that slot machines would begin to become the casinos' main profit center.

By the mid–Eighties, slot machines had matched table games in popularity, and by the time the decade turned, the so-called "one-armed bandits" had clearly become the casino's favorite game. Today, more than two-thirds of casino revenue in the United States is actually derived from the slot machine. Those same casino executives didn't try to change the trend, however. They were delighted that slot

machines were exhibiting such popularity. After all, the money derived from slot machines is preprogrammed and absolutely guaranteed, while table game revenues are subject to the ebb and flow of Lady Luck.

Sure, casinos have the advantage at the table games, but because the games themselves are volatile, the money won or lost on a monthly basis can vary widely.

So slot machines became their cushion, with table games generally making up the difference between a great month or simply a good month.

The casinos can count on slot machine revenues because the machines are simply computers. The profit can be programmed into the machines by the use of a random number generator that determines just how much of the money played in that particular machine will be returned as winnings.

So why should casino customers play the slot machines, since the casino is guaranteed to win? The same random number generator that provides the casino with its guaranteed profit, also gives the player the opportunity to win.

SETTING UP THE PAYBACK

Where did slot machines come from, and how have they achieved the remarkable popularity we see today?

Although the first slot machines were manufactured on the East Coast of the US, they didn't start to gain acceptance until they had migrated all the way across the country to San Francisco around the end of the last century. In the saloons and brothels of the notorious Barbary Coast and the Tenderloin districts in America, customers won a cigar or a free drink when they played a nickel in the primitive slot machines, which at that time used playing cards as winning symbols. Few of the players understood the math in use on the reels of those devices, so the proprietors raked in enormous profits.

There were many slot manufacturers in those days, but only one is credited with creating the "modern" slot machine that included spinning reels and cash payouts. Charles Fey, a German immigrant, invented the "Liberty Bell" slot machine in 1899 that stands as the template for every machine built from then to the present day.

The three-reel design was copied by many other manufacturers, and by 1905, thousands of slot machines could be found in the US, in cigar stores, barber shops, saloons, and bowling alleys.

The Liberty Bell was a simple machine to explain. Each reel operated independently of the other, and stopped one after the other. Each reel had ten symbols or "stops". As a result, there were 1,000 different combinations (10 x 10 x 10 = 1,000). Three specific symbols had to be lined up in order to win the jackpot, which meant there was only one way to win out of 1,000 possibilities. This same basic principle lies behind all modern slot machines.

The early machines were often rigged to prevent the big jackpots from hitting, but even this fix didn't prevent the growing popularity of the aptly named "one-armed bandits".

The San Francisco earthquake of 1906 destroyed the factories of every slot manufacturer, but, along with the rest of the city, the slot builders returned after the destruction with even greater force. But when preachers and holy-rollers blamed the earthquake on God's wrath over the sins of the city, slots were outlawed in San Francisco in 1909, and soon after in all of California and Nevada.

To skirt the law, slot manufacturers disguised their machines as "gum" machines that would dispense packs of gum for jackpots. To further camouflage the machines, the playing card symbols were replaced by fruit—cherries, lemons, oranges, peaches, etc—and labels of the gum brands dispensed, that evolved into the "bars" on today's slot machines.

The imposition of Prohibition in 1918 ushered in the return of illegal slots and the lure of banned liquor and gambling caused an explosion of slots during the Roaring Twenties. The "Golden Age" of the slot machine ended quickly when Prohibition was repealed in 1934. Except for Nevada, where gambling of all sorts was legalized in 1931, slot machines were illegal and not tolerated all across the whole of America.

A mini-revival of slot machines was enjoyed after World War II, until Congress passed the Johnson Act, which banned slot machines in all states which hadn't legalized gambling as a whole.

TODAY'S SLOTS

Even in Nevada, slot machines were merely a curiosity, with even the largest casino containing no more than a few hundred machines. They were there to entertain the browsers, while the serious gambling was conducted at the tables.

A couple of things happened in the 1960s and 1970s that changed the attitudes of both the casino executives and the players. Electro-mechanical machines were developed by pinball-machine builder Bally Manufacturing which permitted many more payoffs than the mechanical machines could accommodate. And the Bally machines came complete with an enlarged "hopper", or coin storage unit, that could hold up to 2,500 coins. In addition, the Bally machines could accept more than one coin at a time, which allowed the players to insert up to five coins on one pull of the handle.

When casinos were legalized in Atlantic City, riverboats in the Midwest and on Indian reservations across the US, slot machines became the game of choice.

Sound effects, special lighting, music and more frequent payouts drew more and more players to the slot machines. Players could chose from three, four, and five-reel machines, and in 1980, Bally engineered a group of advanced machines that could be linked together to create a giant jackpot. Ironically, this development would fuel the growth of Bally's chief competitor, IGT, which developed the "life-changing" million dollar jackpots now commonplace in systems like "Megabucks", "Quartermania", and "Dollars Deluxe".

Today, there are dozens of slot manufacturers around the world, including Australia's Aristocrat, Japan's Universal and Sigma, Europe's Novomatic, and many companies based in the United States. Slot machines are often designed for specific markets. In Australia, Aristocrat produces video slot machines that include intricate graphics and complicated payouts for a very sophisticated slot player. In Japan, pachinko and pachisuro parlors reward players with prizes rather than cash. American players vary according to the area in which they play. In Las Vegas and Atlantic City, mature slot players turn more frequently to video poker, where they feel they have some control over their wins or losses. In other, newer, jurisdictions, the simpler the machine, the better. But the fact remains that slot machines are becoming increasingly popular, and slot manufacturers are producing more attractive machines to entice increasingly selective slot players.

TIGHT vs LOOSE

Slot players are always searching for machines that pay off more than others. These machines are known as "loose" machines, and casinos that offer machines that pay off more than those in other casinos are known as loose casinos.

In the US, gaming regulatory agencies in various jurisdictions publish what is known as the casino "win" on various slot machines. The casino win is the percentage of money deposited in the slot machines retained by the casino as profit (although it is not really profit, since it does not include rent, electric costs, employee salaries, and other costs of doing business). Some agencies identify the individual casinos, while others only name the specific regions. By turning these numbers around, you can identify the "payback percentage", or the percentage of money returned to the player for the money played.

For instance, if a casino "win" is 10 percent, the payback percentage is 90 percent; if the casino win is 12 percent, the payback percentage is 88 percent, and so on.

Most jurisdictions have a minimum payback percentage that every machine must reach. However, most machines pay back much more than the minimum percentage, since competition forces them to try to retain customers through higher paybacks.

Tight machines, on the other hand, are those that don't pay out as frequently as other machines.

The exact definition of "loose" and "tight" is very subjective. One machine may be loose for a short amount of time for a particular player, and tight during a different period for another player. Casinos set the win percentage of each machine as a function of the win percentage for the entire casino. Stated elementally, if a casino wants to establish a 10 percent win percentage on its 200 slot machines, it could set 100 for a 15 percent win percentage, and the other 100 machines for a five percent win percentage. Over the long run, therefore, the machines will produce an overall 10 percent win. Of course, the machines are more likely to be set at graduated percentages so that each machine may be no more than two or three percent different from another. And the win percentage will be balanced for play, since some machines get played more than others because of their locations or style.

In most cases, casinos will direct the manufacturers of the slot machines to install the computer chip that establishes the payback percentage for that particular machine. Only rarely will the casino adjust the payback percentage while the machine is already installed on the casino floor.

But remember, even if you could identify the exact payback percentage of a particular machine, there is no guarantee that you would win over the short term. The payback percentage is programmed into the machine to be effective over thousands and millions of plays. A machine that pays

back 100 percent, for instance, would simply allow the player to break even over the long run. Depending upon the machine's program, it might pay back a large jackpot once, while limiting other paybacks to small, infrequent hits. So you can never tell when a machine is ready to pay off. Should the machine not pay off for several hours, there is no guarantee that it will begin to pay off any time soon.

The payback percentage of machines generally increases with the denomination. Five-cent machines usually carry the worst payback for the player, with the $1 and above machines giving the players the best chance. The reason for this is that it takes many nickels for the casino to make a substantial profit, while it takes only a few dollars to earn a comparable amount. The casino also encourages higher denomination players to play more dollars, and a higher payback percentage will help to accomplish that goal.

Even with a high payback percentage, however, the casino advantage will eventually grind down even the best player. Suppose you had 100 $1 tokens as a bankroll. The following chart will show how the slot machine will gobble up your stake each time you play that stake, assuming that the machine pays back at the exact win percentage every play.

THE EFFECT OF THE INEXORABLE HOUSE EDGE

PLAYS	99% RETURN	93% RETURN	8% RETURN
0	$100.00	$100.00	$100.00
1	$99.00	$93.00	$88.00
2	$98.01	$86.49	$77.44
3	$97.03	$80.44	$68.15
5	$95.10	$69.57	$52.77
10	$95.10	$69.57	$52.77
15	$86.00	$33.67	$14.69
20	$81.79	$23.42	$7.75
25	$77.78	$16.30	$4.09

You can see that the higher the payback percentage, the longer you can play, and the better chance you have of hitting a jackpot that will make you a winner. Even the difference of a few percentage points in the payback percentage can make a big difference in how the machine performs. Stretching your money for the longest possible play session is the key to becoming a winner on the increasing popular slot machines.

FULL COIN PLAY

Multiple-coin machines have several different definitions. On a single-line machine, the player inserts from one to five coins. If a winning combination occurs on the reels with three coins in, the payoff will be three times as much as with one coin in. Four coins will produce a payoff of four times that of one coin, and so on.

Another version of a multiple-coin machine is one with multiple lines. By depositing additional coins, the player activates additional lines that pay off if the winning combinations hit. Some machines even pay on diagonal lines. This type of machine is an enticement to get the players to increase the amount of their wagers. For instance, if a player is only playing one coin, activating only one line, and a winning combination is hit on a non-activated line, it would encourage the player to deposit additional coins in order to have a chance at winning on those additional lines.

In both cases, the payback percentage and the house advantage of the machines do not change whether the player deposits one coin or multiple coins. The amount of profit the casino makes will increase substantially if it can get the players to deposit more than one coin every play.

You should always gamble only what you can comfortably afford, so you should avoid playing five coins if you can only afford to play one, even if the casino tries to entice you with attractive paybacks. The only reason to play the full amount of coins would be if the slot machine rewards you when winning the top jackpot.

For instance, if one coin pays ten coins for a particular winning combination, two coins pay 20 for the same combination, and three coins pay 50, it would be to your advantage to play three coins. The disparity in the awards makes it worth it.

But if you can't afford to play those three coins, it's advisable to find a machine that makes an evenly graduated payback for multiple coins, or drop down to a lower denomination.

SLOT CAROUSELS

Most casinos have sets of slot machines that are grouped by denomination called carousels. They usually have a theme that is designed to attract a certain kind of player. In Nevada, casinos advertise carousels with a higher payback, by using a slogan such as "Up to 97 percent payback". The disclaimer is the "up to" phrase, which means that only a few machines in the carousel may pay back as high as 97 percent.

Carousels are sometimes linked together to calculate a progressive jackpot. These types of machines differ because the top jackpot is not a set amount, but increases as players deposit more money. For example, the top jackpot may increase five cents for every dollar played in the carousel. Every machine contributes to the jackpot, and the first machine to hit the jackpot symbols wins the award.

When the jackpot is won, the top award reverts to the minimum amount that is determined by the casino.

The Megabucks and Quartermania-style slots are machines that are linked together between different casinos. The jackpots on these machines can reach the multi-million dollar level, much higher than individual casinos would be able to offer.

The machines are linked to a central computer by 'phone lines, allowing the machines to communicate with the computer that eventually determines when the winning combination will be hit.

If you want to play progressive machines, deposit the maximum number of coins, because you are not eligible for the top jackpot unless you do. Imagine how painful it would be to hit the winning combination and only have one coin in. Instead of winning, say, $5 million, you'd only win $5,000. It's one of the few instances where winning would hurt.

FIVE TIPS FOR SMART SLOT PLAY

While you now understand how a slot machine works, and how the percentages rarely work in your favor, there are some ways to approach slot machines that might make your experience more enjoyable…and profitable.

The following are five tips that aren't necessarily supported by numbers, but can't hurt when you consider how and which slots to play.

Ask for help: That's right, you don't have to guess about which machine to play. You have a resource at your fingertips. Ask the slot personnel on the floor. Ask the change people who work the slots, or who stand inside one of the carousels handing out change. They do nothing but watch slot play in their casino all day long, so there's a good chance they at least have an idea about which machines pay off. They may tell which machine they think is the right machine, or which one is due to hit. They could be wrong, but they want to help you win, because if you do, there's a chance you'll give them a tip.

Walk the floor: Take a few minutes after you arrive to watch the play of other players and to look at the patterns of the machines. Note which ones have paid a jackpot, or those that always seem to be ringing and buzzing. Knowing machines can be helpful, the same way a craps player waits around for a table to get hot.

Play the top number of coins: In most cases, you win big when you hit the jackpots. And the jackpots on most machines, especially progressives, jump to bonus levels when you play the maximum number of coins. Don't miss out on this by being a coin short when you hit.

Reserve your favorite machine: If you have found a machine that is lucky for you, and you want to continue playing after a short break, the change person will reserve it for you for a short time while you leave the floor. Just ask them for help and give them a small tip for doing so.

THE SLOT SLANT

The slot department on the casino floor can be a confusing place. Hundreds of different machines greet the player. Bright colors, mindless electronic tunes and flashing lights seem to assault the senses. Different pay tables and payoff percentages; straight payoffs or progressive slot systems; win-a-car prizes or take the money and run; the choices are tremendous. Just making a decision about which machine to play often seems to be daunting.

The following quiz may clear up some of the confusion that faces a prospective slot player when deciding on where and what machines to play:

1) Can you win playing a slot machine?
Yes. Slot machines are set to pay back a certain percentage. In New Jersey, by law, slot machines must pay back 83 percent of the money played. In Nevada, it's 75 percent. Most major properties in each jurisdiction, however, pay back much more than that. But even at 75 percent, a player can hit a lucky streak and go home a winner. Sure, most players may not win anything, but there are plenty who do win if they know the secret. Somebody's got to get lucky.

The key to beating the slot machines is to quit while you're ahead. Money management is sometimes an overused term in the gamblers' world, but it applies here. Set a reasonable win goal. If you have a budget of $100, don't try to double your money. The chance of that happening is remote. Quit when you get $25 ahead. Go enjoy a show. Get a meal. Or simply watch the other players. And when you get home, you can say you beat the casino.

2) How many coins should I play? Won't my money last longer if I play one coin at a time?
Yes, your money will last longer, but by playing only one coin, you're giving up the chance of either hitting the big jackpot, which usually pays a bonus for playing the maximum amount of coins, or you're not activating all the lines on a multi-line machine, therefore excluding yourself from the chance to hit more frequent jackpots.

Always play maximum coin. If you can't afford maximum coin at the $1 machines, drop down to 25-cent machines. But whatever you do, don't miss out on the chance to win the big or frequent prizes.

3) How can you tell which machines pay out more than the others?
Checking the payback of the casinos in the areas you plan to visit gives you a head start. These are often published in

local newspapers or casino publications. Unless you have a favorite casino where they know you personally and you feel comfortable, why not head for the casinos with the highest payouts? It only makes sense.

It gets a little more difficult when you get to the casino. You can't tell which machines pay more than others just by looking at them. It takes study and intuition.

First decide upon your gaming budget. To play $1 machines, you should have at least a couple of hundred dollars. If you've got less than $100, head for the quarters.

Then take a walk around. Check out the action. Try the three-pull rule: Put the maximum number of coins in the machine three times. If you hit a small jackpot, keep playing. If you don't get anything back, move on. You'll know when you're comfortable and things are flowing.

Play the machines at the end of the aisles that are near other banks of slot machines. Sources say that slot executives place higher paying slot machines in locations that are visible to other players so that they will lure players to other, lower paying, slot machines.

Avoid slot machines surrounding the table games. Table players may get up to stretch and drop a few coins in a nearby machine. Casino executives don't want those table players to get lucky and continue to play the slot machines instead of the table games, so they put the tightest machines around the tables.

Likewise, avoid machines near the showroom or food outlets where people wait in line. Since these players merely drop a few spare coins into the machines with no expectations of winning, there's no reason for the casino to put loose machines in those locations.

If you're still confused, ask a slot attendant which machine pays off more than the others. They work the slot floor all day long. Maybe they'll steer you to a machine that they see pay out more than others. If they help in this manner, don't forget them. Slip them a few bucks, and you've found a friend for life.

4) Can the casino change the payback on a machine whenever it wants?

The answer is a qualified "yes". When a casino buys a slot machine, it will tell the slot manufacturer to deliver it already programmed to pay back a certain percentage. Unless there is a major change in the slot marketing policy of a casino, the percentage will not change.

If a casino does decide to change the payback percentage (and when they do this, it's usually done to increase the payoff, rather than decrease it), it is done over a period of several weeks so the change will be gradual.

5) Is it better to play a machine with a progressive jackpot or one that has lower paybacks?

It depends upon your objective. If you want to go for the life-changing jackpot—something that will allow you to tell your boss where he can put your job—a slot machine with a big progressive jackpot will give you a thrill. The chances of hitting that jackpot are quite remote, to say the least, but it will no doubt be exciting to dream about it.

If you want to have a chance of taking home a little more money than you arrived with, you might want to concentrate on the machines that offer lower, but more frequent, payouts. The way to determine which machines fall into this category is to read the glass. Check for multiple payout combinations and you're probably in the ballpark.

6) What is a random number generator?

The random number generator (RNG) is the heart of the slot machine for the player's purposes. This little computer chip determines how much the machine pays out by constantly cycling through numbers and producing combinations that comply with the payoff percentage desired by the casino.

7) Aren't slot clubs just a way for the casino to make sure you don't win too much money?

Slot clubs have very little to do with winning or losing. The card readers attached to nearly every modern slot machine allow casino management to compile data on the players. It tells them how much the customers play, what denomination, how many coins per pull they deposit and, yes, how much they win or lose.

How much a player wins is not the issue here, however. Casinos know that statistically they will win a set percentage from each player over the long run…and they mean the l-o-n-g r-u-n. A player could beat a casino every day for a year, and it wouldn't change how the casino treats that person. A slot club is used to determine how many goodies (rooms, meals, shows, cash back) a casino can give individual players as a reward for their loyalty. It only makes sense to register for the slot club in a casino before you play so you qualify for its incentive programs.

8) Why do some states in America require that a machine be shut down for a period after it hits a big jackpot?

Today's slot machines are electro-mechanical wonders, with safeguards built into them to prevent tampering. But slot cheats are only one step behind even the most advanced slots technology, so when large (or even smaller, hand-paid) jackpots are hit, the casino will want to examine the machine to make certain the jackpot was hit honestly, and not through some type of malfunction or player tampering. So not only do the regulatory agencies generally require it, but the casino also wants to verify the jackpot to protect itself against fraud.

9) Most progressive slot systems (Megabucks, Quartermania, Pokermania) pay out their jackpots over a 20-year period. What happens if the casino goes out of business during that time? What are the payout percentages for these systems?

In the case of the Megabucks, Quartermania, Fabulous 50s, High Rollers and other multi-casino linked slot systems, the manufacturer and supplier of these systems, International Game Technology, maintains a trust system. Let's say a player hits a $1 million jackpot. IGT and the system's participating casinos will deposit an amount of money in a bank account that will spin off $1 million over a 20-year period. The amount of money they deposit depends upon the prevailing interest rate, but the player is guaranteed to receive the whole $1 million over the course of 20 years. Even if all the casinos and IGT went bankrupt during that period (not a very likely possibility), the jackpot winner will still receive their prize.

The participating casinos in a linked-slot system get together to decide on the payoff percentage. In Nevada, for instance, the payoff percentage for Megabucks in March 1994 (the latest available data) was 87.8 percent.

When the jackpot is hit, the percentage will soar to the upper 90s or more. But averaged out for the entire year, Megabucks pays less than the typical $1 machine (89.4 percent Vs 95.7 percent). Generally, the same is true of all the progressive linked systems.

Some linked systems, by the way, pay the entire jackpot all at once. Bally's Bucks, in Atlantic City, and Fastest Cash, at the Circus properties in Nevada, are just a couple of examples of such systems.

10) How can you tell when a machine is due to hit?

A word that should not be in any slot player's vocabulary is "due". No machine is ever "due". The RNG constantly cycles and conceivably could pay out two top awards in the space of two pulls, and then not pay another for years.

The only way to even get an idea about individual machines is to "scout" them over an extended period of time. Keep mental (or even written) notes about which machines you and other players seem to win on again and again.

Those machines that pay out consistently will be the ones on which to concentrate your play. No, it's not an exact science, but even a little information can go a long way.

THE SLOT CHART*

The following chart is a typical month for US casinos and the payback percentages they offer at their slot machines. The loosest slots in the US are located in the Downtown region of Las Vegas in Nevada, with a 95.4 percent payback. You'll notice that the poorest payback percentages are located mostly in Atlantic City. But many of those paybacks are augmented by programs that reward frequent gamblers, such as cashback programs, free rooms, food, gifts and other promotions. Although it appears that your money goes a longer way in Nevada and some of the other areas, when you figure the "extras", Atlantic City casinos are usually comparable. Also note the 101.1 percent payback percentage at Casino Rock Island in Illinois. Occasionally, you'll see this anomaly, which indicates that a casino paid out more than it took in for one month. This will be balanced out over the course of a year.

ATLANTIC CITY	25¢		50¢		$1		$5		TOTAL	
April, 1995	# Slots	Win %	# Slots	Win %	# Slots	Win %	# Slots	Win %	# Slots	Win %
The Grand	1046	90.4	224	91.2	437	91.6	91	95.1	1,834	91.6
Bally's Park Place	1,358	90.1	268	92.1	429	91.8	82	95.0	2,237	91.7
Caesars	1,062	88.9	375	89.7	542	91.5	75	93.7	2,121	91.1
Claridge	1,194	89.9	176	90.3	313	91.2	15	94.4	1,734	90.4
Harrah's AC	1,052	91.1	279	91.2	595	92.5	80	94.8	2,022	92.3
Resorts	1,195	89.3	375	90.9	422	90.8	51	95.5	2,056	90.8
Sands	1,173	89.9	266	90.1	465	91.6	78	94.5	1,992	91.1
Showboat	2,266	91.1	220	90.2	425	91.8	47	94.0	3,045	91.4
Tropworld	1,534	92.1	376	92.2	695	92.5	107	94.9	2,804	92.6
Trump's Castle	1,248	90.0	339	91.0	460	92.3	77	94.0	2,209	91.2
Trump Plaza	1,392	89.7	284	90.9	479	91.5	73	94.7	2,324	91.0
Trump Taj Mahal	2,285	90.3	354	91.3	645	92.0	98	94.7	3,540	91.4

NEVADA	25¢		50¢		$1		$5		TOTAL	
February, 1995	# Slots	Win %	# Slots	Win %	# Slots	Win %	# Slots	Win %	# Slots	Win %
Downtown	3,002	91.7	8,556	95.6	2,720	95.6	199	96.2	14,847	95.4
LV Strip	5,337	89.2	21,598	93.9	8,832	95.2	903	95.7	37,754	94.5
Laughlin	2,726	88.1	7,132	94.6	2,701	95.9	248	96.1	13,101	94.7
Lake Tahoe	920	90.0	3,537	94.6	1,787	95.3	234	95.8	6,685	95.0
Reno	1,860	92.4	4,881	94.1	2,624	95.9	233	96.7	9,852	95.2

ILLINOIS	25¢		50¢		$1		$5		TOTAL	
March, 1995	# Slots	Win %	# Slots	Win %	# Slots	Win %	# Slots	Win %	# Slots	Win %
Alton Belle II	–	–	409	92.0	207	94.9	20	96.9	636	94.0
Par-A-Dice	21	83.5	485	91.1	269	93.0	15	94.7	793	92.3
Casino Rock Island	–	–	296	91.6	90	93.4	5	101.1	393	92.8
Joliet Empress	–	–	457	90.3	436	94.7	56	95.7	964	93.8
Silver Eagle	21	83.4	335	90.7	107	92.7	7	93.6	472	91.7
Metropolis Players	20	86.6	430	88.6	204	91.9	18	94.1	672	90.9
Harrah's Joliet	–		420	90.7	357	95.2	57	94.3	961	93.9
Hollywood	–	–	314	90.9	234	94.5	42	95.5	706	93.5
Casino Queen	–	–	559	92.5	344	95.2	19	95.6	922	94.3
Grand Victoria	–	–	506	91.5	404	95.1	56	95.5	1,006	94.5

CONNECTICUT	25¢		50¢		$1		$5		TOTAL	
April, 1995	# Slots	Win %	# Slots	Win %	# Slots	Win %	# Slots	Win %	# Slots	Win %
Foxwoods	2,032	90.7	604	91.8	1,094	92.5	108	93.9	3,864	92.0

IOWA	25¢ §		50¢		$1		$5		TOTAL	
April, 1995	# Slots	Win %	# Slots	Win %	# Slots	Win %	# Slots	Win %	# Slots	Win %
President	46	NA	504	NA	190	NA	11	NA	776	93.0
Missisippi Belle II	51	NA	288	NA	102	NA	3	NA	440	92.6
Diamond Jo	22	NA	211	NA	93	NA	6	NA	332	92.5
Catfish Bend	NA	NA	NA	NA	NA	NA	NA	NA	260	90.7
Belle of Sioux City	–	–	NA	NA	NA	NA	–	–	441	90.5
Miss Marquette	NA	NA	NA	NA	NA	NA	NA	NA	620	89.3
Lady Luck	NA	NA	NA	NA	NA	NA	NA	NA	785	91.1

COLORADO	25¢		50¢		$1		$5		TOTAL	
March, 1995	# Slots	Win %	# Slots	Win %	# Slots	Win %	# Slots	Win %	# Slots	Win %
Cripple Creek	878	90.5	2,004	93.2	719	94.3	52	94.2	3,686	93.4
Black Hawk	714	90.4	2,495	93.5	1,129	94.0	86	94.7	4,461	93.7
Central City	654	89.2	2,181	92.5	943	94.8	66	96.1	3,844	93.2

MISSISSIPPI	25¢		50¢		$1		$5		TOTAL	
March, 1995	# Slots	Win %	# Slots	Win %	# Slots	Win %	# Slots	Win %	# Slots	Win %
Coastal Region	2,293	88.5	7,110	90.8	3,365	93.7	304	95.6	13,680	NA
North River Region	1,037	87.2	6,488	91.1	3,550	94.6	381	95.6	12,133	NA
South River Region	357	87.9	1,825	91.4	1,041	93.4	92	95.6	3,393	NA

*As it was noted previously; in the United States, some gaming, regulatory agencies in the various gaming states issue monthly reports on casino revenues. Within those reports are listed the casino "win" at slot machines, which means how much money the casino retains after all bets are paid. For simplicity's sake, say the casino had a slot 'handle' of $100 million. If at the end of the month, the casino retained $10 million, it had a 10 percent win percentage. That means the slot players won $90 million, or had 90 percent payback percentage. While some regulatory agencies identify the specific casinos, others only designate a certain region where casinos are located. In Europe, there is little precedent for reporting casino revenues so it is difficult to gauge a specific payback percentage for any casino or region. In general, however, casinos with competition will generally offer a higher payback percentage than those with a monopoly or those that are isolated.

THE SYSTEMS APPROACH

FINDING WINNING MACHINES

Jim Wilson makes a monthly excursion to Caesars Palace. He flies from his home in suburban Chicago and spends a long weekend in Las Vegas, taking in shows, betting an occasional sporting event, but mainly playing the slots. Jim knows that Caesars Palace is known for its high-limit table game players, but has come to realize that in most cases slot players are valued just as highly by the casinos. With a gambling budget each trip of about $1,000, Jim can play for hours each day, and still have a good chance of winning.

Slots are not like table games where a player can estimate the house edge and play accordingly. On slot machines, a player never knows what the house advantage is. It can vary anywhere from 2 percent to 30 percent.

Jim made the most important move the first time he came to Caesars Palace. He joined the Emperors Club, Caesars' club for slot players. He received his players' club card, which he inserts in the card reader available at every Caesars Palace slot machine. That way, his play is recorded by the casino, and he becomes eligible for the various levels of complimentaries the casino provides to its better players.

When Jim arrives, he divides his $1,000 bankroll into four lots of $250, one for each of his four-day stay. He then divides that daily bankroll into five sessions of $50 each. That way, Jim is not held hostage to a brutal losing streak, and will not lose his entire stake during one gambling session. Jim's next step is to decide what machines to play. In most cases, dollar machines will pay back at a greater rate than 25¢ machines. But should he be unlucky, his session stake will disappear more quickly at the dollar machines. He also knows that his Emperors Club points pile up at a much faster rate on the dollar machines. Jim feels confident, however, so he chooses the dollar machines.

Being a frequent player, Jim realizes that there are several different varieties of machines, aside from the brands and themes. Multi-casino, linked progressive slot machines offer huge paybacks that can reach as high as $10 million. While those machines are attractive, and their overall payback percentage may be comparable to other $1 machines, unless a player wins the big jackpot, the payouts are infrequent and small. Other single-casino progressive machines offer high jackpots, but the payback percentages are again weighted toward the big payout, and smaller jackpots are less likely. So Jim opts for the machines that offer smaller top awards, but pay out more frequently. That gives him a better chance to break even or possibly win a bit.

Jim's next step is a little less than scientific, but he has used it to good success. "Scouting the slots" as Jim calls it, allows him to take note which slots seem to be more active. If he sees a player winning steadily, he mentally notes the type and location of machine, and later may return to that spot to try it himself.

While a "hot" machine can be explained as the computer program cycling through a payback period, Jim also knows that some machines are set at a higher payback than others. It therefore follows that certain machines permanently pay off more than others. Jim has found this to be the case on many occasions.

Another tool that Jim uses is the slot attendants, the employees who work the slot section. Jim knows they work long shifts with nothing else to do but watch the slot machines. On many occasions, he has asked a slot attendant to steer him to a machine that is "due". While it doesn't always work, it has paid off often enough. Jim now has "friends" in the Caesars Palace slot department who understand that when Jim hits a jackpot on a machine they recommend, they get a hefty tip.

Jim finally settles in at a $1 machine, and begins to play. He always inserts the maximum coins because he doesn't want to lose out on the bonus paid when the top award is hit with full coin in.

After falling behind, he begins to make some small hits until he enters the "plus" column. At every session, Jim sets a goal of 20 percent. When he wins $50, he quits. He then puts the $300, in an envelope and mails it home. He won't be tempted, and he'll leave Las Vegas without having lost everything.

CHAPTER 9

VIDEO POKER

POKER, THE VIDEO VERSION

How video poker gives a skilled player the chance to get the best break at any gambling machine. Possibly the best way to get money out of the casino without using illegal methods.

Before reading this chapter, forget all you've read in the previous chapter on poker—except for the ranking of poker hands. Video poker is not live poker, and outside of how you evaluate the hands, it bears little resemblance to the table game.

Video poker is a fairly recent phenomenon, dating back to only the mid Seventies. Although early slot machines used cards and poker hands as payoff symbols, players had no choices to make; the reels stopped wherever the machine determined they would.

The increasing popularity of video poker can be traced to several factors and characteristics it has in common with many of the more popular casino games. For instance:
- It's fast (like craps).
- It gives players the opportunity to make decisions and a reasonable control over the results (like blackjack).
- It's similar to poker (like many of the newest casino games).
- It gives the possibility of a large payoff and is not intimidating (like slot machines).
- You can play it for a low minimum, an investment as small as a nickel.

Maybe what makes it even more popular is that it returns your investment for a pair of Jacks to Aces. In effect, this makes the player feel like a push (a tie) is a win. This is an important psychological factor that makes it seem like you're winning more than you actually are. Maybe it's because when you drop a coin into the machine, you consider that a lost coin, so that when it reappears on an even-money payoff, you feel like you're a winner. It's a subtle point, but a powerful one.

Perhaps the chief reason that video poker is becoming more popular is that even a casual player can determine the value of an individual machine. By simply glancing at the pay table included on every video poker game, you can determine how much that machine will pay back to players who use the optimal video poker strategy, or expert strategy.

Playing winning video poker requires three very important tenets. First, you should only play machines that give you the highest payback. Second, you must know how to use the best strategies to play those machines. And finally, you should be aware of how those machines reach those payback percentages. That is, you must be aware of whether that payback percentage is reached by awarding a single large jackpot or whether it encompasses many smaller paybacks. It's called the volatility of the machine, and how frequently payoffs are made.

Many machines can be played to pay back more than 100 percent of the money invested. How is this possible, you ask? Isn't the casino going to lose money by putting these types of machines on the floor?

This question has two answers. Yes, the casino would lose money if every player on that particular machine understood and used expert strategy. But since only a small minority of video poker players truly know how to take advantage of such a machine, no, the casino will not lose money by offering such a machine. And even if it was just expert players that were attracted to such a machine, they wouldn't all be able to play at the same time. Therefore, the casino would undoubtedly surround that machine with others offering a significantly lower payout than that single 100 percent-plus machine, guaranteeing the casino the chance to win more money from those other players.

FINDING THE BEST MACHINES

When video poker was first introduced, few people realized that the pay tables would play such a large role in determining how much and how frequently the machine made payoffs. Since serious players began to analyze the pay tables, it has become apparent that choosing the correct machine to play makes all the difference.

There are generally two types of video poker games—non-wild card games, such as Jacks-or-better and Bonus Poker, or wild card games, like Jokers Wild and Deuces Wild. While this is a general classification, there are many versions of these machines, and that's why it is so important to understand what makes a good pay table.

To begin with, let's concentrate on the non-wild card games. The first rule of thumb is never play a machine that does not return your investment on a high pair—a pair of Jacks to Aces. Although these machines are thankfully disappearing, it used to be common to find machines that required the players to make two pair before returning their bet. This is an unacceptable option, and there really is no need to play these machines given the proliferation of Jacks-or-better machines.

Let's examine a Jacks-or-better pay table. This is usually located above the screen, and it generally gives you the payoffs for the number of coins inserted, usually from one to five. On most modern machines, the pay table is located on the screen itself, just above the area where the hands appear.

Look at the various rewards. You'll notice the hands correspond with the poker hands we discussed earlier in the book. But because you're not playing against opponents, you get paid back at a progressing rate beginning with the high pair.

The area you should concentrate on is the payoff for the full house and the flush. The best machines are ones that pay nine coins (for one coin) on the full house, and six coins for the flush. This is called a "9/6" machine. This machine, of course, is preferable to an "8/5" machine that pays eight coins for the full house and five for the flush. Other machines—7/5 and 6/5 machines—are far less favorable and should be avoided unless there is no other choice.

Bonus poker is a relatively new variety of the game that increases payoffs for different four-of-a-kinds, at the expense of a full house and a flush. The best bonus poker machines offer a payback of eight for the full house and five for the flush. Machines that don't reach that level have a lower payback percentage.

One other factor is important when choosing the best video poker machines. Las Vegas, and other areas in Nevada, are video poker heaven, where you'll find the best and most generous pay tables in the casinos in the Silver State. Generally, these machines cannot be found anywhere else.

Atlantic City is improving, but finding 9/6 machines requires a diligent search because very few casinos offer them. On the other hand, Atlantic City is far superior to most riverboat or dockside casino jurisdictions or Indian casinos for a couple of related reasons. Most of these new casinos cater to relatively new players, who usually gravitate to the slot machines because they are not intimidating, and it takes little knowledge to play them. When they do wander into the video poker area, they are generally not educated in the game, so the slot executives have little reason to offer them the best paybacks. Even if a player is educated, he most often has no alternatives. In Las Vegas or even Atlantic City, if you don't find a machine with a favorable payback, you can go next door and have a better than even chance of finding it there. If you try that on a riverboat, you'll be taking a very unexpected swim. The point is that there is little competition for educated players, so there is no incentive for casino executives to offer high-paying video poker machines.

EXPERT PLAY PAYBACK PERCENTAGE

Players can obtain a high payback percentage by using expert strategy on the following types of video poker machines. The key to each machine is the return for one

MACHINE	9/6	8/5	6/5
Royal Flush	*800*	*800*	*1,000*
Straight Flush	*50*	*50*	*50*
Four-of-a-Kind	*25*	*25*	*25*
Full House	*9*	*8*	*6*
Flush	*6*	*5*	*5*
Straight	*4*	*4*	*4*
Three-of-a-Kind	*3*	*3*	*3*
Two Pair	*2*	*2*	*2*
Jacks-or-Better	*1*	*1*	*1*
Payback Percentage	*99.5%*	*97.3%*	*95.5%*

coin on the full house (9, 8 or 6) and the flush (6 or 5).

PROGRESSIVE POTS

Another twist in video poker paybacks is a progressive jackpot. These incorporate a progressive meter above a carousel of video poker machines, and a portion of each bet is designated to fund the progressive jackpot that is usually hit on a royal flush.

When a bank of Jacks-or-better machines offers a progressive jackpot, you won't find 9/6 machines because the top award accounts for a larger percentage of the overall payback percentage. But don't be fooled by being attracted to a big progressive jackpot when the payoffs for a full house and a flush aren't at a reasonable level. You're not getting the best bet unless you play at an 8/5 machine on a regular Jacks-or-better game.

Professional video poker players know that when the progressive meter hits $2,200 on a quarter video poker machine, they have the edge. Often a team of players will occupy every seat on such a carousel until the jackpot is hit.

IGT, the company which developed the Megabucks, Quartermania and Dollars Deluxe linked slot systems, has had some trouble developing a similar system for video poker. Because the players can actually play for a royal flush when the progressive jackpot reaches high levels, professional players could actually make it more likely that they'd hit the big jackpot. Requiring the winning hand to be "sequential"—that is lined up from Ten to Ace left to right or vice versa—didn't work, either, because the professional player could alter his style to go for that jackpot as well.

At one point, IGT developed what they called Star Poker. The random number generator added stars to the cards that make up a royal flush, and the players couldn't predict when or where those stars would appear, so they couldn't alter their playing style to try to win the progressive jackpot. But because it was so confusing, it wasn't very popular.

Today, there is a system called Pokermania that designates a suit for each machine. For instance, a player sitting at a machine designated for diamonds must hit a sequential royal flush in diamonds to win the progressive jackpot. If he draws a sequential royal flush in hearts, he gets a good payoff, but not the progressive. These machines seem to satisfy the player, but are still not as popular as the slot versions of the giant progressive jackpots. And because you're supposedly playing for the big jackpot, you pay a big price in the full house/flush payout. Rarely will you see a giant linked progressive jackpot video poker system paying more than six for a full house and five for a flush.

STRATEGIC
MISTAKES

Once you've identified the good machines and decided to sit down and play, the next step is to use expert strategy. Don't expect to play flawlessly the first time you sit down.

Because the different machines all have their own special strategies, you should stick with one type of machine until you've thoroughly understood and mastered its specific expert strategies.

Once again, Jacks-or-better is the most basic choice, and by mastering its expert strategy, you'll have a better chance at the more complicated strategies of other video poker machines. The following strategies can be used for progressive Jacks-or-better and even bonus poker without losing much of an edge.

The most important concept to grasp at the beginning is the need to eliminate costly mistakes. Most of those mistakes are made by confusing video poker with live poker, and can be generalized as follows:

● **Don't hold a kicker.** *A kicker is an unpaired high card that you would hold along with a lower pair. For example, if you have:*

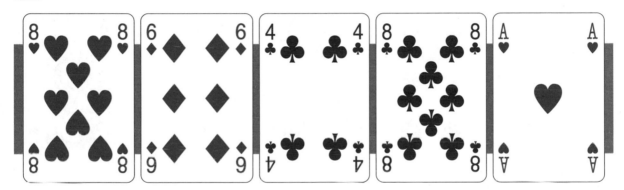

don't hold the pair of Eights along with the Ace. When playing live poker, that play can be made occasionally to throw your opponents off the trail. But you can't bluff a machine. Holding a kicker reduces the chances to improve the pair which is more valuable.

● **Don't draw to an inside straight.** *This is good advice whether you're playing live or video poker. It seems to be a particular failing of video poker players, however. If you draw:*

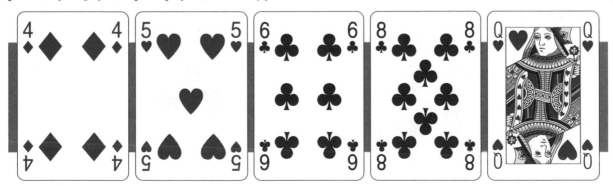

you've only got one chance in 13 of filling that straight if you discard the Queen.

Only draw to a straight when it's open at both ends. A hand like:

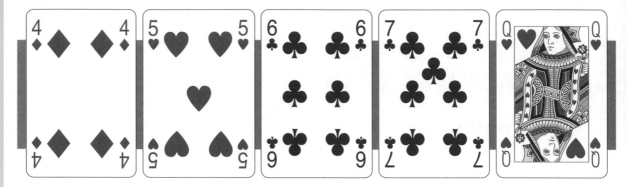

can be made by discarding the Queen and drawing either a Three or an Eight.

● Don't hold three cards hoping to draw a flush. *The odds of drawing two cards after discarding to complete a flush like:*

are prohibitive, and will destroy your expert strategy.

The same holds true for a straight. Don't hold:

looking to draw cards to fill in the straight. The odds are you won't.

An exception is drawing two consecutive suited cards. For example:

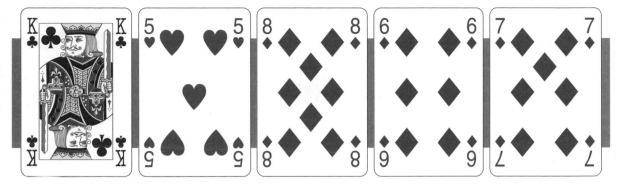

is close enough to a straight flush that it makes a decent risk for a high payoff.

● *Don't play two-card connectors. A hand like:*

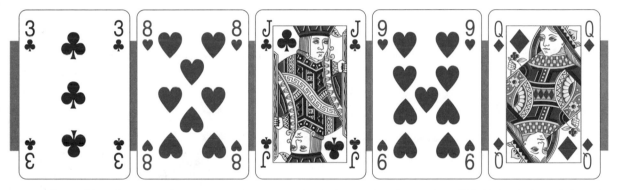

is virtually worthless, but many players seem to be enamored with the suited quality, and would hold the Eight and Nine of Hearts. The chances of drawing a straight flush or even a straight is too remote to make this play a viable option.

MAKING IT COUNT

With over 25 varieties of high-pair machines—Tens, Jacks and Kings or better—documented in the past five years, it's difficult to designate an overall expert strategy, but there are some common suggestions that will keep you in the game much longer than if you simply "fly by the seat of your pants". These are applicable to most of the Jacks-or-better and bonus poker games, and will give you the best chance to walk away a winner.

● *Hold any pair, high or low, rather than keeping one or two high cards, even if they are suited. For example, if you have:*

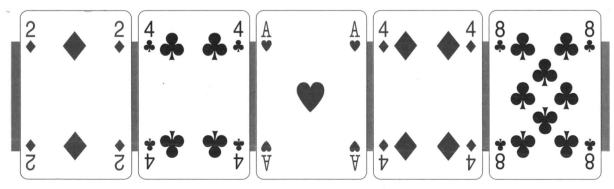

hold the Fours. Forget about the Ace. The Fours give you the best chance of achieving a winning hand.

And don't be tempted to hold two high cards, even if they are suited and connected.

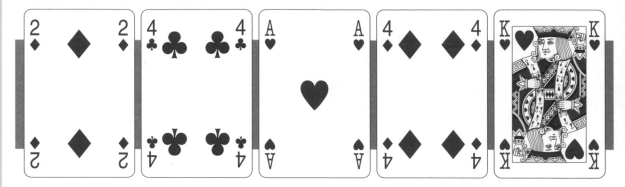

The Fours are still your best bet by far.

● *If you don't have a pair, hold any card above a Ten to a maximum of two. For example, in a hand like:*

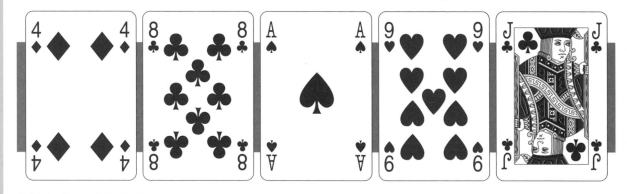

hold the Ace and the Jack.

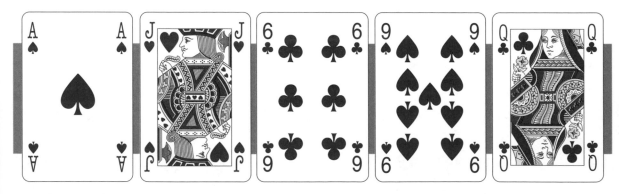

If you have three high cards, hold only two, and hold the lower of the high cards because you have a better chance of making a straight. Hold the Jack and the Queen. The Ace is the least valuable of the three high cards.

If two of the three high cards are suited, only hold the suited cards:

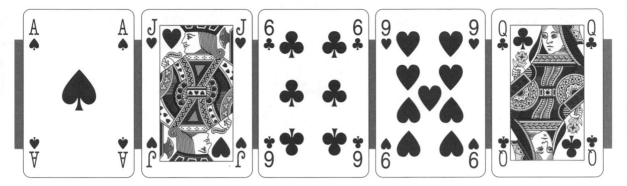

Hold the Ace and Jack of spades. You'll have the best chance at the royal.

When confronted with confusing hands that seem to offer chances at different high-paying hands, use a ranking system. Hands like:

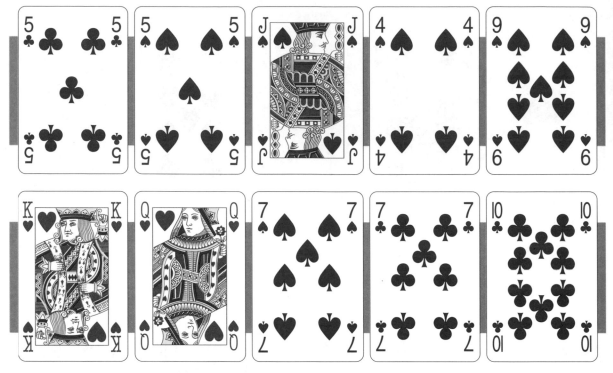

create all sorts of problems. You must choose between high or low pairs, missing the chance at straights or flushes, or drawing two to a royal flush.

To help sort out these decisions use the following system to decide the priority of the various hands:
High pair
Three-card royal
Four-card flush
Low pair
Four-card straight

Using this ranking, the play in the first example would be to hold the Queens. In the second example, go with the low pair. In number three, split the low pair, and go for the flush, and finally, go for the royal.

● Keep all five cards in a straight or flush rather than discard to go for the straight flush. For example:

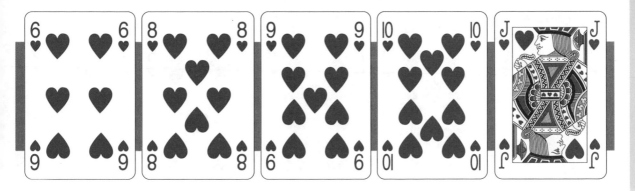

Each of these hands are already winners, and discarding the Ten of Diamonds in the first example and dropping the Six of Hearts in the second represent too high a risk. Stick with a winner.

● *Break up a straight or flush to go for a royal flush. For example, in the two hands:*

you have a legitimate chance to draw a royal flush. The difference between the payoff on a royal and one on a straight or a flush is large enough to sacrifice a winner. Go for it!

127

● *If you don't have a low pair:*

a high card:

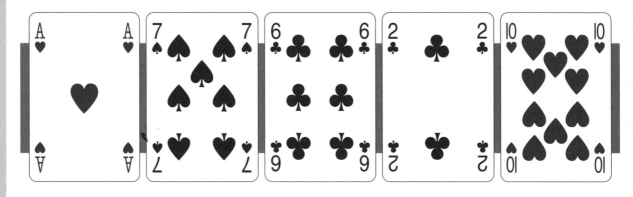

a one-card draw to a flush:

a one-card draw straight open at both ends:

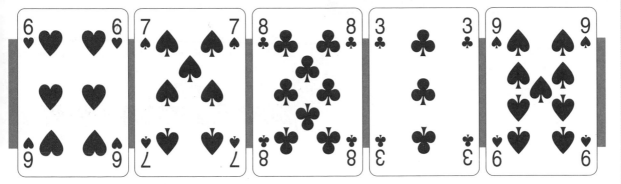

or three consecutive, suited low cards:

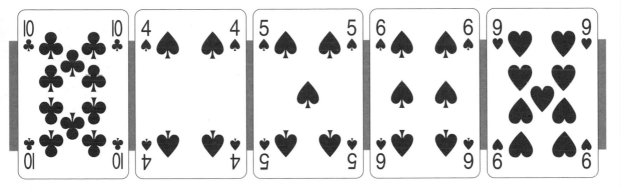

discard them all and draw five new cards.

Please remember that this strategy is simply an overall guide for Jacks-or-better. Depending upon the machine you choose, there are additional decisions that will affect the overall payback. You'll need to buy some books or consult some magazines, as well as invest in playing time to discover these alternate strategies.

DOUBLE YOUR MONEY

Some video poker machines have an option that allows you to risk the winnings on a hand for a chance at doubling your money. While many players believe that this is simply another ploy by the casino to take your remaining stake, it's actually one of the best bets in the casino. It's exactly 50-50 that you will be able to double your money. No house edge; no tricks. So what's the catch?

You may double as many times as you wish, and because the odds are even, you'll eventually lose. It's a risk the casino is willing to take, but by examining the law of diminishing returns, it's one that will be risky for the player.

While each decision is exactly 50-50, the odds of winning more than one in a row decrease sharply. After the first hand, you're not gambling on the individual hands, you're gambling on the sequence, and that is stacked heavily in the casino's favor.

DOUBLE YOUR RISKS

From the Double Your Risk chart, you can see that the chances of winning your double diminish the more times you attempt to buck the odds against the sequential wins. The odds against winning ten in a row before you begin to double is less than one tenth of one percent. Not very good odds, although the odds against winning any individual double down is 50-50.

Some players will try to suggest that the machine "knows"

NO. OF DOUBLES	ODDS OF WINNING	CASH AT STAKE AFTER WIN
1	50.00%	$10
2	25.00%	$20
3	12.5%	$40
4	6.25%	$80
5	3.13%	$160
6	1.56%	$320
7	0.78%	$640
8	0.39%	$1,280
9	0.19%	$2,560
10	0.09%	$5,120

when you are doubling a high win. That's nonsense. You can see that the casino wants you to try to double as many times as possible, and there is no need to "rig" the machines. You're already bucking some pretty big odds for more than two in a row. The casino is very happy to offer you 50-50 odds on each bet.

Try it at your own risk.

A SMALL QUIZ

You've seen the basic expert strategy for a 9/6 Jacks-or-better video poker machine. Let's see if you can play a few hands that will show you what you'll encounter when playing in an actual casino. Play the following hands by discarding the cards that will give you the best chance at a winning hand and compare them with the correct plays to find out if you're ready to tackle the real thing.
Answers at the end of the chapter

The video poker problems (right) are just a cross-section of the hands you can expect to receive when playing an actual machine. Check the following rating to find out if you are ready for the big time casino action:

20-26 correct: **Expert**—You should be able to at least break even on your first attempt, and you might even be a winner.

15-20 correct: **Apprentice**—You've made a good start at understanding the basics, and are ready to take a small step at the casino's video poker department.

10-15 correct: **Student**—You're learning, but must take some time to study the reasons behind your choices.

Below 10 correct: **Loser**—Don't even think about entering a casino. Mail your money in, or better yet, buy a computer so you can practice, practice, practice on a machine that won't cost you any money.

	1	2	3	4	5
A	JD	10D	JC	KD	8S
B	10C	5D	6H	4H	9S
C	AH	QS	KS	JH	4D
D	10D	JD	3C	8C	8D
E	5C	7C	10H	QH	KD
F	4S	9S	10S	JS	QS
G	AS	6C	3S	JH	KD
H	JH	QH	9H	4S	4C
I	JH	8C	5C	2D	4C
J	JC	4S	5S	7S	QH
K	QH	4S	6S	JH	5S
L	JS	QD	6H	4H	5H
M	10S	KS	4H	5H	7H
N	AD	JS	4C	6C	8C
O	7H	6H	5C	4H	10D
P	QH	4S	8H	2D	9H
Q	10D	4S	5C	6S	7S
R	JH	10H	7H	3C	6S
S	QC	10C	AS	5S	7D
T	10S	5H	AS	7S	JH
U	8S	AH	10D	QS	KS
V	2S	JD	QD	KC	10S
W	AS	2D	10H	JH	KC
X	QS	QH	3H	6H	10H
Y	3H	9H	KC	5D	JS
Z-BONUS	AH	QH	JH	10D	KH

THE MEANINGFUL ONE

It's only one card, but what a difference it makes! With 53 cards in the deck, the different possibilities for winning hands in Joker Poker are very appealing to slot players who enjoy video poker. When that Joker appears on the screen, it adds an immediate bonus.

The explosion in the popularity of video poker slot machines has understandably led to the development of games that use wild cards. The Joker Poker slot machine is the most popular of these games. It adds a 53rd card to the deck for each hand. Since this gives the player more opportunities to draw winning hands, and indeed, makes the game easier, the payout schedule is lower than ordinary video poker.

The Joker will come up about ten percent of the time and the player must be prepared to react to certain situations in a different manner to how he would in an ordinary video poker game. Strategy changes in this game and the different situations must be understood to take advantage of the higher payoffs.

Though there are many different types of Joker Poker machines—most pay only on two pair, others pay for Jacks-, Kings- or Aces-or-better—and pay tables vary, the strategies in the accompanying table are applicable to most situations. In Atlantic City and some riverboats, the highest jackpot is for five-of-a-kind. In Las Vegas, the royal flush cops the top award.

The Joker can be used as a substitute for any other card, or used as a fifth imaginary card of any value (to complete a five-of-a-kind hand, for instance). The machine automatically computes the best hand when using the Joker. The only exception to this rule is that the Joker cannot be used to complete a royal flush (Ace, King, Queen, Jack, Ten of the same suit). A Joker completing this hand is paid off as a straight flush. In most versions of Joker Poker, the lowest payoff is two pair, unlike many video poker machines that pay off for Jacks or Better.

There are some basic rules that apply only to Joker Poker. These guidelines are formulated by the unique situations and odds that exist by the addition of the one wild card.

Never draw more than three cards, regardless of the first five cards received. If you get a Joker in the first five cards, always keep one additional card to start with a pair, before the draw. If you don't have a Joker, keep at least two cards of the same suit, so you at least have the beginning of a flush. Drawing a royal flush is not possible when you get a Joker in the first five cards, so any flush will be paid off, at best, as a straight flush.

When you start with a Joker, you can't finish with two pair. It's simple.

With the Joker, partial straights are better than partial flushes. If you have a Joker-Seven-Eight-Nine any Five, Six, Ten or Jack will pay off. That is 16 possibilities. For a four-card flush with a Joker, you only have ten possibilities to complete that flush. Though the payoff for a straight is slightly less than for a flush, you will draw a straight more times than a flush.

Winning at Joker Poker is no more difficult than an ordinary video poker machine. Joker Poker is, however, much more complicated and you must understand what the addition of the wild card does to the probabilities. This very challenge makes Joker Poker more exciting.

Give it a try.

JOKER POKER STRATEGY

The following rules are the correct basic strategy to use when playing Joker Poker. Best hands are listed first. When you are dealt the Joker:

1 *Stand with five-of-a-kind or a straight flush.*
2 *Draw one card to four-of-a-kind.*
3 *Stand on a full house.*
4 *Stand on a flush.*
5 *Draw one card to a four-card straight flush.*
6 *Stand on a straight.*
7 *Draw one card to any four-card inside or double-inside straight flush.*
8 *Draw two cards to three-of-a-kind.*
9 *Draw one card to a four-card straight.*
10 *Draw two cards to a three-card straight flush.*
11 *Draw one card to a four-card inside straight.*
12 *Draw one card to a four-card flush.*
13 *Draw two cards to a three-card inside straight flush.*
14 *Draw two cards to a three-card straight.*
15 *Draw two cards to a three-card double inside straight flush.*
16 *Draw one card to a to a four-card double inside straight flush.*
17 *Draw three cards to a pair.*

When you are not dealt the Joker:

1 *Stand with a royal flush or a straight flush.*
2 *Draw one card to four-of-a-kind.*
3 *Stand on a full house.*
4 *Draw one card to four-card royal flush.*
5 *Stand on a flush or straight.*
6 *Draw one card to a four-card straight flush, either open-ended or inside.*
7 *Draw two cards to three-of-a-kind.*
8 *Draw one card to two pair.*
9 *Draw one card to a four-card flush.*
10 *Draw two cards to a three-card royal flush.*
11 *Draw one card to a four-card straight.*
12 *Draw two cards to a three-card straight flush, either open-ended or inside.*
13 *Draw three cards to a pair.*
14 *Draw three cards to a two-card royal flush.*
15 *Draw one card to a four-card inside straight.*
16 *Draw two cards to a three-card double-inside straight flush.*
17 *Draw three cards to a two-card straight flush, open-ended, double-inside or triple-inside.*
18 *Draw two cards to a three-card flush.*
19 *Draw two cards to a three-card straight.*
20 *Draw three cards to a two-card flush.*

DIGGING THE DEUCES

The other popular wild-card video poker game is Deuces Wild. Because it has four wild cards, it complicates the strategy that is necessary to succeed at the machines.

Just as in other varieties of video poker, it's important to note the pay table on Deuces Wild. But it's not as easy as with Jacks-or-better. Casino executives have discovered several different ways to alter the pay tables that will alter the payback percentages.

DEUCES WILD PAYBACK PERCENTAGES
The pay tables below are just three examples of Deuces Wild games available today. The small variations in the pay table are the reason for the variation in payback percentage for expert play.

WORKING THE DEUCES
The object of Deuces Wild, obviously, is to obtain the wild

Royal Flush	800	800	1,000
Four Deuces	200	200	200
Deuces Royal	25	25	25
Five-of-a-Kind	15	16	15
Straight Flush	9	13	9
Four-of-a-Kind	5	4	4
Full House	3	3	3
Flush	2	2	2
Straight	2	2	2
Three-of-a-Kind	1	1	1
Payback Percentage	100.6%	96.8%	94.3%

cards to get those valuable hands. But what does it mean when you start off the hand with Deuces?

Even in the highest paying version of Deuces Wild—at 100.6 percent—you will receive No Deuce hands 66 percent of the time, which means that 80 percent of your hands will be losers. Another 14 percent will be the minimum three-of-a-kind winner, which is actually just a push. So if you don't get a Deuce before the draw, you will actually win only six percent of the time.

When you get one Deuce in the initial hand—only 30 percent of the time—45 percent of your hands will be losers, and another 38 percent will get the three-of-a-kind push, leaving only 17 percent that will actually win. Another nine percent will be near-minimum winners as straights and flushes. Two Deuces in the initial hand—dealt only four percent of the time—means that you must take every advantage of this hand, despite the fact that 70 percent of these hands will wind up being flushes or lower. About one in four will end up as four-of-a-kind, and one in 98 will wind up as five-of-a-kind.

DEUCES STRATEGY
The following strategy is a little more complicated than the other two versions covered in this chapter. Some basic rules are not to play any machine that does not pay five-for-one for four-of-a-kind. And most important of all, even if you've got a shot at a natural royal, do not discard any Deuce!

1 *Stand with any natural winning hand, except for a natural straight flush starting with Nine. Discard the Nine and go for the royal.*
2 *Draw one card to a straight flush.*

3 *Draw one card to a royal flush.*
4 *Draw two cards to a royal flush.*
5 *With two pair, discard one pair and draw three cards.*
6 *Draw one card to a flush.*
7 *Draw one card to a straight.*
8 *Draw two cards to a straight flush.*
9 *Draw three cards to a Queen-Jack, Ten-Jack, or Jack-Ten suited.*
10 *Draw two cards to a suited Six-Seven and a Deuce.*
11 *Draw one card to a three-card royal and one Deuce.*
12 *Draw one card to a four-card straight with one Deuce.*

13 *Stand on any winning hand with one Deuce. Break up a flush, straight or three-of-a-kind for any four-card royal flush, or four-card straight flush.*
14 *Draw one card to a suited Six-Seven or better with two Deuces.*
15 *Draw one card to a four-card royal with two Deuces.*
16 *Draw one card to four-of-a-kind with two Deuces.*
17 *Stand on five 10s or better with three Deuces.*
18 *Stand on royal flush with three Deuces.*
19 *Stand on five-of-a-kind with four Deuces.*
20 *All other hands discard everything but Deuces.*

THE SYSTEMS APPROACH

PLAYING MAXIMUM COINS

Ellen arrived at her favorite casino with a group of friends at about noon, but it hasn't been her day. Ellen is an avid video poker player, and understands that she should always play the maximum coins. Coin limit play is essential, she believes, because if she hits the royal flush, she wants to be eligible for the top award that winners who have the maximum coin in receive. After all, the pay tables on most modern machines are set to offer the coin-limit player a better payback percentage by setting a higher jackpot on the top hand for coin-limit play. Most machines start the hand automatically when five coins are inserted. Every machine has one button that orders maximum play. Ellen believes that it is the only way to play.

But Ellen's bankroll has been depleted and she believes it's time to drop down to less than coin limit to stretch her remaining bankroll. Ellen has seen players who have been burned by hitting a royal flush or five-of-a-kind while playing less than coin limit. The disdain from the neighboring players was more difficult to bear than the monetary shortfall.

But before coming to the casino this time, Ellen read up on coin limit play and was surprised to find that on her favorite 9/6 Jacks-or-better machines, she would be losing less per hand by playing one coin than by playing five coins.

By playing expert strategy, and even taking into account the 800-for-one payout for five-coin play and only a 250-for-one payoff for anything less, Ellen can take solace in the fact that her single-coin play keeps her almost even with maximum play, even without the hitting the top jackpot.

Ellen wasn't so surprised to find that novice players who don't understand expert strategy are much better off playing less than five coins. Her friends who love the slots have occasionally wandered over into the video poker sections, but have always headed back quickly. They don't understand that it's important to know the strategy of the game.

Progressive jackpots would seem to demand coin-limit play, but Ellen learned that a typical progressive 8/5 Jacks-or-better machine pays only 97.3 percent to experts when the jackpot is minimum at 800 for 1, or $1,000 on a five-quarter coin-limit machine. Single-coin play returns only 95.9 percent so the loss rate is very poor at all levels. That's why experts don't play them until the jackpot is above $2,200 and then only at coin-limit. Ellen will continue to play one coin at a time until it's time to head home with her friends. She'll protect her bankroll and will even have a chance to get even before leaving.

CHAPTER 10

EXOTIC GAMES

FOR OTHER CASINO GAMES, BUYERS BEWARE

The Casino, as well as being a home to the most famous games in the world is also a haven for some of the more obscure recreations. Most of these 'exotic' games should be avoided, but there are exceptions.

Casino gambling should be approached with caution, even when you understand the pros and cons of the "big five" casino games. As you have seen in this book, blackjack, roulette, craps, baccarat and poker each have something going for them when a reasonably skillful player considers what game to play. Even slots and video poker can be played with a reasonable expectation that a player can win with a little luck.

But these aren't the only games offered in a casino. There are several mainstays that are offered in virtually every casino, unfortunately there are some very good reasons to avoid them. Yet more games are constantly being introduced at an impressive clip as casino executives try to lure players back to the tables. But while they are trying to make table games ever more attractive by adding gimmicks and twists to existing games, casino executives are overlooking—or ignoring—an important point. The house advantage on almost all the new games introduced over the past five years is more than 2.5 percent for each game. If new games were launched that had a reasonable house edge, educated players may be more receptive to them. It's the chance of winning you get at blackjack, craps and the other games that made them popular to begin with.

BASIC BIG SIX

The Big-Six wheel (also known as the wheel of fortune) is one of the easiest casino games to play, but also the one in which the casino enjoys its largest edge. The huge wheel spins lazily as players place their bets on a large table with money symbols covered by a sheet of glass. The wheel contains 54 slots, each represented by a number, usually symbolized by US greenbacks—$1, $2, $5, $10, $20, a joker and the casino logo. There are, of course, many more $1 symbols than there are jokers, and the payoffs take this disparity into account.

The minimum bet is $1, and the maximum varies according to the denomination of the bet. Bets are made by purchasing chips or—only in Nevada—laying money on the table. If you bet on the $1 symbol and it wins, you get paid 1-to-1. If you bet on the $2 symbol and it wins, you get paid 2-to-1; a $5 win gets you 5-to-1, and so on. The joker and casino logo pays 45-to-1 (40-to-1 in Las Vegas), but they are each separate bets; if the joker wins, the casino logo loses. The player may bet on one number or any combination of numbers on each spin.

In some casinos, two dealers are used to deal the game. One dealer spins the wheel and the other watches the table as the first dealer turns to call the winner. All bets must be made before the wheel is spun. When the dealer calls "no more bets", he can accept no further wagering. In Atlantic City,

chips may not be rested on the side of the table and hands must remain back from the table layout.

In some jurisdictions, only one dealer is used, and a mirror on the table allows him to call a winner without taking his eyes off the table. In any jurisdiction, Big Six is a bad game. If for some inexplicable reason you must play, play the $5 bet in Atlantic City or the $1 bet elsewhere. But if you really have to play find a carnival or Boardwalk. You'll have much more fun and you might even win a furry stuffed animal.

BIG SIX ODDS AND PAYOFFS

SYMBOL	OCCURRENCES ON WHEEL	PAYOFF	CASINO EDGE
$1	24 [23]	1:1	11.1% [14.8%]
$2	15	2:1	16.7%
$5	7 [8]	5:1	22.2% [11.1%]
$10	4	10:1	18.5%
$20	2	20:1	22.2%
Joker	1	40:1 [45:1]	24% [14.8%]
Casino Logo	1	40:1 [45:1]	24% [14.8%]

N.B. Figures in [brackets] indicate Atlantic City

DON'T COUNT ON KENO

Everyone has played those giant lotteries sponsored by state or provincial governments. The jackpots reach millions of dollars (pounds or whatever your native currency) but the odds of winning are astronomical. In most cases the odds reach into the tens of millions to one. But when the jackpots reach double figures in millions, the fantasy of winning that jackpot almost always overwhelms our knowledge of the odds against winning. After all, we reason, someone has to win; why can't it be me?

The casino has a game that has a similar attraction, with odds that aren't much better. Keno advertisements showcase jackpots of $50,000 and more for matching all 20 numbers picked in any one drawing. For a bet of $1 or $2, you might be tempted to use the same reasoning; someone has to win it. But in a casino, someone doesn't have to win it. In fact, someone rarely wins it.

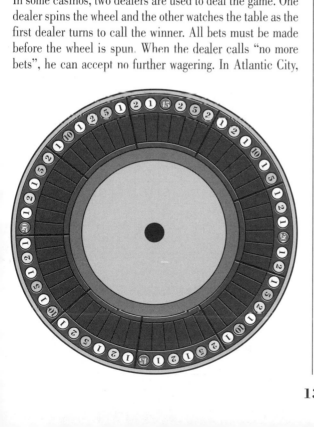

Let's look at what it takes to win a multi-million dollar lottery. In most cases, you only have to pick all six numbers chosen. Most jurisdictions give you a field of 40 numbers to chose from. Others have as many as 54. You'll see that keno is even more difficult to win.

Originating in China, the game was brought to the US by Chinese immigrants building the transcontinental railroad. The game soon caught on with Americans and, for some reason, Omaha, Nebraska became the keno capital of the US. But when gambling was banned in Nebraska, Nevada took over the game, and today it is offered in virtually every casino jurisdiction.

Although many games are conducted electronically today, Nevada keno games still use ping-pong balls being blown around in a large clear plastic sphere. The balls are then forced into a "goose", an outlet which takes one ball at a time.

In casino keno, the house draws 20 numbers out of a field of 80 numbers. You can choose as few as one number or as many as 15. To make your bets, you fill out a keno ticket, which has boxes for all 80 numbers. The casino provides a "keno crayon", which you use to mark your numbers. Choosing individual numbers in this manner is called a "straight" keno ticket.

Minimum bets are as low as 50 cents, but most casinos accept bets of $1 or more. The game can be played from virtually anywhere on the casino property. Keno runners, employees who take bets, circulate throughout all the areas of the casino and hotel to give you the chance to make a bet on each game. Numerous television monitors keep you informed of the winning numbers.

The payoffs vary from casino to casino, as well as for the number of choices made, and the number of those choices that actually hit. For instance, if you bet eight numbers and five come up, you get an 8-to-1 payoff. But if you pick five numbers and all five come up, you get a 485-to-1 payoff. Each number is called a spot, so if you choose five numbers, the ticket is called a "five-spot" ticket.

Because the casino edge on keno is astronomical—between 25 percent and 40 percent, depending upon the numbers played—you might think it makes more sense to pick fewer numbers, as opposed to picking all 15 possibilities. For instance, if you had picked ten numbers and five hit, you'd only get a 2-to-1 payoff.

A straight ticket is not the only way you can play keno, however. You can bet groups of numbers that give you a better chance of winning. These are called "way" and "combination" tickets. You are given credit for hitting all three numbers if any one of the group hits. Many experienced keno players will use this method for a wider selection of numbers and a better chance to win.

Still, the big jackpot is very elusive. In a typical game, a $10 bet will win the $50,000 jackpot if you choose seven numbers and catch all seven. In the same game, you can win the top jackpot for a $2 bet if you hit 11 out of 11 numbers.

With these odds, you might as well play the million-dollar lotteries. There is one good thing about keno in a casino. You can relax in the keno lounge, an area with comfortable chairs and frequent visits by cocktail waitresses. By simply betting the minimums, you can spend the day being catered to by the casino employees without losing your shirt. After all, generally only six games are played each hour, so you can enjoy the casino atmosphere for a lot less than any other game, even given the horrible odds.

SEEKING SIC BO

Another Chinese immigrant is the game of Sic Bo, which literally means "dice pairs". Although it is Oriental in origin, it is very similar to a popular English game known as Grand Hazard. You'll see that the game is also similar to Big Six in the manner of placing the bets and, unfortunately, the odds.

When you wander up to a Sic Bo game, you might think you've taken a wrong turn into the arcade. The table is an elaborate illuminated affair, with the winning bets highlighted by the illuminated sections.

Sic Bo is really a simple dice game. After all the bets have been made, the dealer spins a small cage containing three dice. Players have made their wagers by placing chips on the sections that designate possible combinations of the results of the dice roll.

The various sections of the table depict the faces of the dice in different patterns. After the dealer shakes the dice, he enters the results into the table, which lights up in the winning pattern. The dealer sweeps the losers from the table and pays off the winners in the amount of the different payoffs.

There are seven different types of bets on the layout of a Sic Bo table. First of all, players may wager on any one of the six dice sides, 1 through 6. If that number comes up on any one of the dice, the player is paid even money. If two of the dice come up with the same number, the bet is paid off at 2-to-1. And if all three of the dice come up on that same number, the bet is paid at 3-to-1. The house edge on this number is 7.8 percent.

The next wager is a combination of two particular numbers. If, for example, a 2-5 or a 3-6 come up on any two of the dice, the bet is paid off at 5-to-1, giving the house a big 16.6 percent advantage.

Bets can also be made on the total of all three dice. The player can bet on any specific total from 4 to 17. The payoff on this bet varies from 6-to-1 to 50-to-1, depending upon the total bet. The house edge can also vary between 9.7 percent to 47.2 percent, a wide differential.

The next bet is a wager of "small" or "big", which means that if you bet on small, you're wagering that the three dice will total between 4 and 10. Big bets win if the dice total between 11 and 17. At first glance, this wouldn't seem like such a bad bet. After all, there are 216 possible combinations on the dice (6 x 6 x 6 = 216), so you could discern that there would be 109 ways to win and 107 ways to lose. But look at the fine print under the small and big bets. It says "lose if any triple appears". That means if three twos or threes or any other three-of-a-kind comes up, you lose, even though the total might constitute a small or big win. That means there are only 105 ways to win and 111 ways to lose. But even with the catch thrown in, the big and small bets are the best at the Sic Bo table, giving the house a rather reasonable 2.7 percent edge.

Let's say you want to hedge your big or small bet and wager that a particular triplet will come up. Bad idea, because the three-of-a-kind bet is among the worst on the table. If you bet, for instance, that three fours will come up, you'll get paid 150-to-1, but the true odds are 215-to-1, giving the casino an almost criminal 30 percent advantage.

Betting any triplet is even worse. You get paid 24-to-1 on this bet, but the true odds are 35-to-1. You're bucking a 30.5 percent house edge.

Want an even worse bet? Try betting that a pair of any particular number will come up. The house pays 8-to-1 on this bet, but you're going up against a nasty 33.3 percent casino advantage.

Sure, Sic Bo is an easy game to play, but if the dice are what

appeals to you, spend a little time and learn how to play craps. If it's the flashing lights, you'll do better playing the slot machines than this terrible game.

SIC BO TOTALS

TOTAL	PAYOFF	CASINO EDGE
4 or 17	60-1	29.1%
5 or 16	18-1	47.2%
6 or 15	14-1	30.5%
7 or 14	12-1	9.7%
8 or 13	8-1	12.5%
9 or 12	6-1	18.9%
10 or 11	6-1	12.5%

DIALING DOMINOES

Yet another game with an Oriental origin is pai gow. The game is played almost strictly by Asians, and the rules and strategy are rather difficult to learn, limiting its appeal to casual observers. The game is played on a blackjack-sized table, and is played with dominoes, not cards (pai gow means "heavenly dominoes"). The 32 specially designed dominoes are "shuffled" by sliding them around the table face down. The dealer then throws three dice to determine which player will start the deal.

All players, including the casino, take turns at being the dealer. Each player, including the dealer, gets four dominoes, which he studies, and then forms into two separate hands; the front, or high hand, and the back, or low hand. The strategy is complicated, but to win, both of the player's high hand must beat the dealer's high hand, and his low hand must be lower than the dealer's low hand. If one wins and the other loses, no money changes hands; it's a push.

Since pai gow is a game of skill, it's difficult to estimate a house edge. The difficulty is confounded by the fact that the dealer banks the game, rather than the casino.

Few occidentals have taken the time to learn the complicated procedures that govern how to set the hands, but there is an American cousin of the game that has taken the casino world by storm.

THE WESTERN VERSION

The introduction of pai gow into the US spurred the development of a similar game, pai gow poker, which uses cards rather than dominoes. It is similar to pai gow in that it is a game of skill, with a front (high) and a back (low) hand. As with pai gow, the player must win both hands to be paid. The hands are easy for non-Asians to understand because they are based on poker hands.

Pai gow poker is actually the only casino game introduced in the past five years that offers the players a reasonable chance to win. Since it is a game of skill, players with a complete understanding of the game have a definite advantage over novice or even intermediate players. Such skillful players can actually gain a long-term theoretical edge over the casino, just like an expert blackjack player can.

The game starts when one player is designated as the dealer/banker, who is responsible for banking the bets at the table. If no one wants to be the banker, the house will act as the banker. The game is played with a standard 52-card deck, with one Joker added which can be used as an Ace. The Joker can also be used to complete a straight, flush or straight flush.

Before the deal begins, the casino dealer shakes three dice, which determines the order of the deal. Each player is then dealt seven cards. The player then must "set" two hands: the back hand, which is composed of five cards, and the front hand, which consists of two. The back hand should always be the stronger hand. If a player accidentally sets a stronger front hand, he automatically loses his bet. If the banker/dealer makes this mistake, however, the casino dealer will re-set the hands according to the casino's policy.

To win, the player's two hands must beat the two hands of the dealer/banker. If only one hand wins, the bet is a push. If both hands lose, the dealer/banker collects the bet. If the player and the dealer/banker have exact hands, it is called a "copy". All copies go to the dealer/banker, and if he wins

PAI GOW POKER

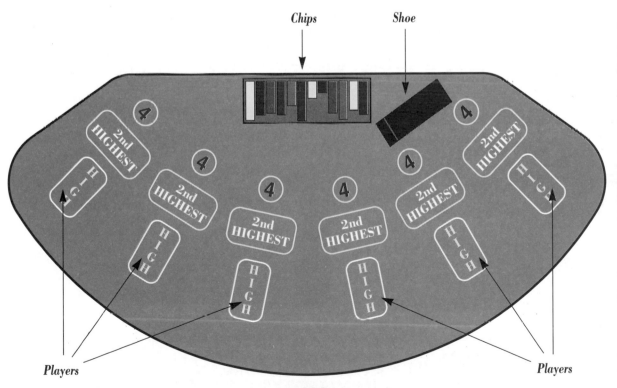

Chips   Shoe

Players   Players

the other hand, the player loses the bet. A "double copy", where both hands are exactly the same, is awarded to the dealer/banker. This, thankfully, is a very rare occurrence and you don't really need to worry about it.

This is the rule that gives the dealer/banker the advantage, and is the reason why, if you decide to play pai gow poker, you should take the opportunity to be the dealer/banker whenever possible. Even though the house takes a five percent commission on all winning bets, acting as the dealer/banker and playing with expert strategy can actually turn the casino advantage toward individual, skillful players. If you don't take advantage of the opportunity to play the dealer/banker role, winning over the long term is impossible. This means that if you play pai gow poker, you will need a bankroll to cover all the bets at the table.

PGP STRATEGY

Unfortunately, there is no hard and fast basic strategy that is easy to understand and just as easy to memorize for this game, as there is in blackjack. But there is a "basic" understanding of how the hands should be set that will give you the best chance at winning. Starting with the worst hand, we will progress to the better hands to demonstrate how best to set the two hands.

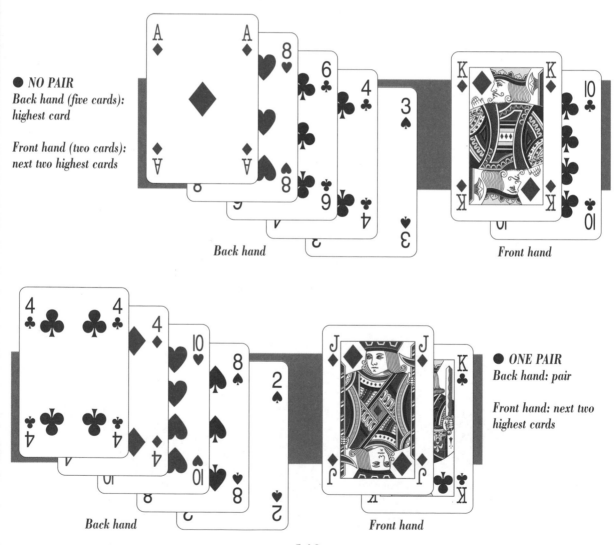

● *NO PAIR*
Back hand (five cards): highest card

Front hand (two cards): next two highest cards

Back hand

Front hand

● *ONE PAIR*
Back hand: pair

Front hand: next two highest cards

Back hand

Front hand

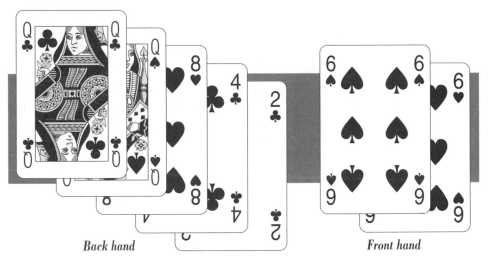

● *TWO PAIR
when high pair is
Queens through Ace
Back hand: high pair*

Front hand: low pair

Back hand   Front hand

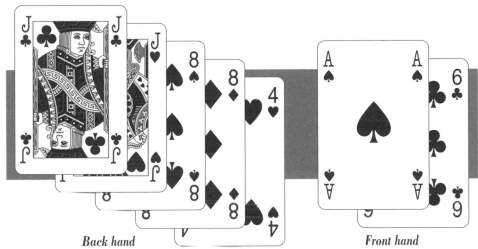

● *TWO PAIR
when high pair is Six
through Jacks, with Ace
or King
Back hand: both pairs*

Front hand: Ace or King

Back hand   Front hand

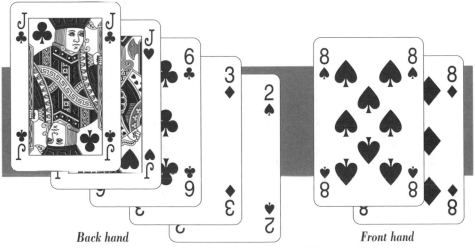

Back hand   Front hand

● *TWO PAIR
when high pair is Six
through Jacks, withou
Ace or King
Back hand: high pair*

Front hand: low pair

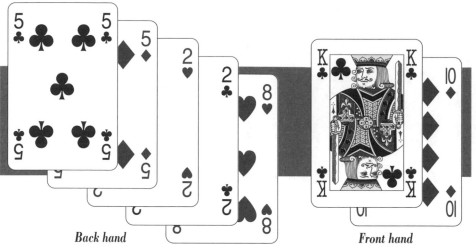

● *TWO PAIR*
when high pair is Three
through Five, with Ace
or King
Back hand: both pairs

Front hand: Ace or
King

Back hand   Front hand

● *TWO PAIR*
when high pair is Three
through Five, without
Ace or King
Back hand: high pair

Front hand: low pair

Back hand   Front hand

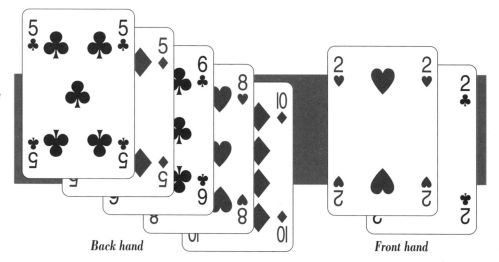

● *THREE PAIR*
Back hand: second and
third highest pair

Front hand: highest pair

Back hand   Front hand

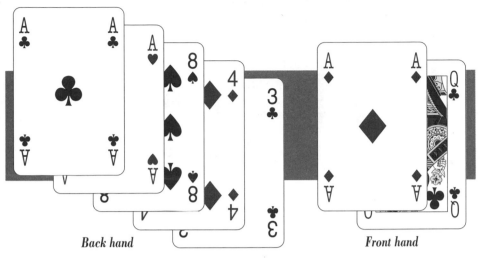

Back hand   **Front hand**

● **THREE-OF-A-KIND:**
   ACES
Back hand: two Aces

*Front hand: one Ace,
next highest card*

● **ALL OTHERS**
*Back hand: three-of-a-
kind*

*Front hand: two highest
cards*

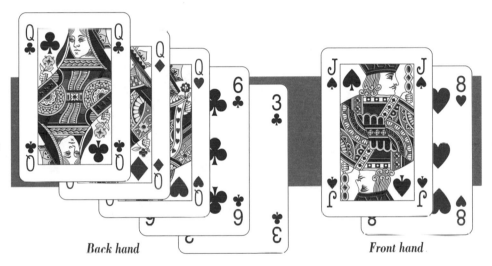

Back hand   **Front hand**

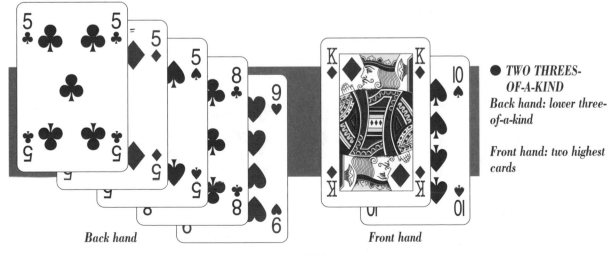

Back hand   **Front hand**

● **TWO THREES-**
   OF-A-KIND
*Back hand: lower three-
of-a-kind*

*Front hand: two highest
cards*

143

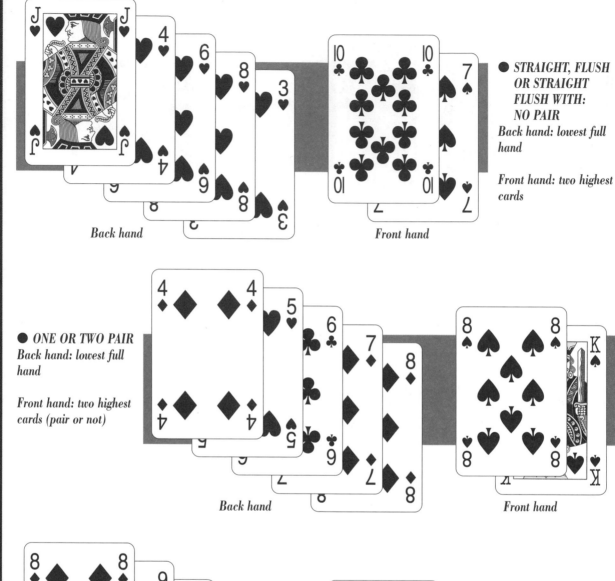

● **STRAIGHT, FLUSH OR STRAIGHT FLUSH WITH: NO PAIR**

Back hand: lowest full hand

Front hand: two highest cards

Back hand

Front hand

● **ONE OR TWO PAIR**
Back hand: lowest full hand

Front hand: two highest cards (pair or not)

Back hand

Front hand

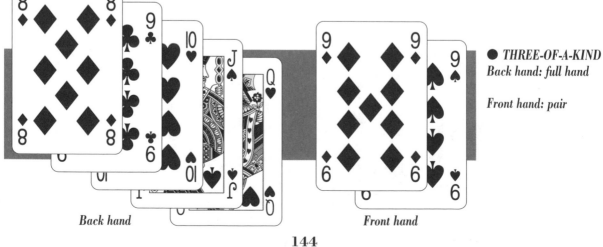

● **THREE-OF-A-KIND**
Back hand: full hand

Front hand: pair

Back hand

Front hand

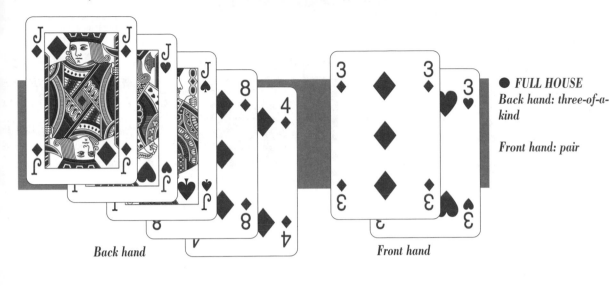

● **FULL HOUSE**
Back hand: three-of-a-kind

Front hand: pair

Back hand   Front hand

● **TWO THREES-OF-A-KIND**
Back hand: lower three

Front hand: highest two

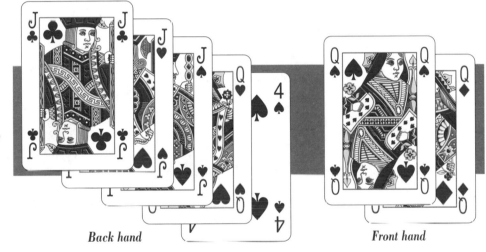

Back hand   Front hand

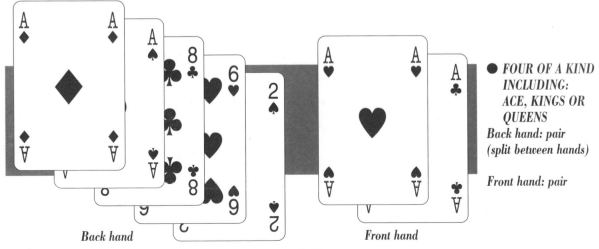

● **FOUR OF A KIND INCLUDING: ACE, KINGS OR QUEENS**
Back hand: pair (split between hands)

Front hand: pair

Back hand   Front hand

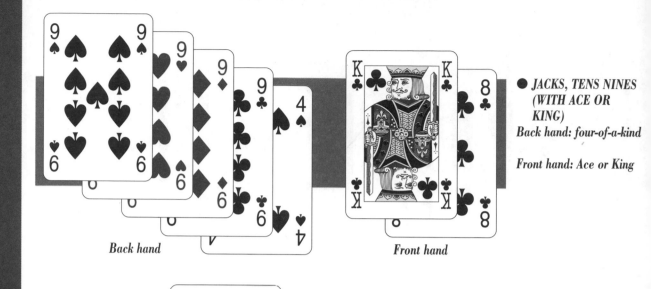

● **JACKS, TENS NINES (WITH ACE OR KING)**
Back hand: four-of-a-kind

Front hand: Ace or King

Back hand   Front hand

● **JACKS, TENS OR NINES (WITHOUT ACE OR KING)**
Back hand: pair (always split between hands)

Front hand: pair

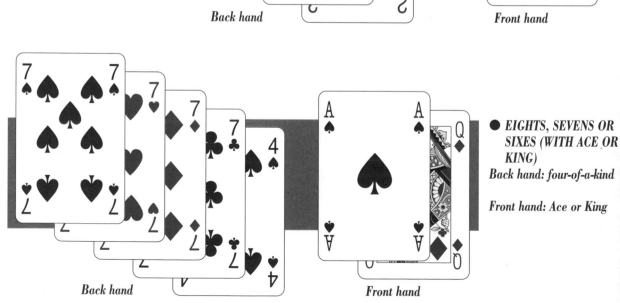

Back hand   Front hand

● **EIGHTS, SEVENS OR SIXES (WITH ACE OR KING)**
Back hand: four-of-a-kind

Front hand: Ace or King

Back hand   Front hand

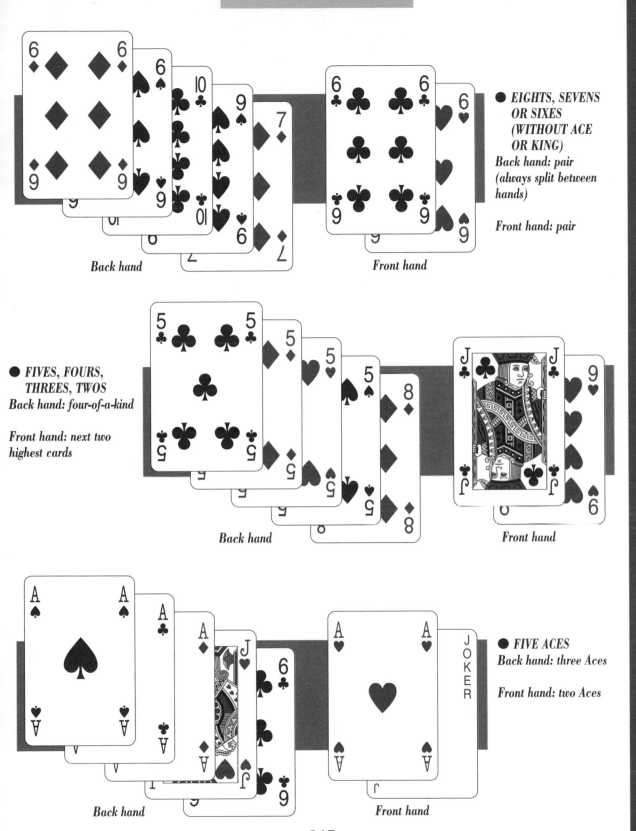

● *EIGHTS, SEVENS OR SIXES (WITHOUT ACE OR KING)*
Back hand: pair (always split between hands)

Front hand: pair

Back hand   Front hand

● *FIVES, FOURS, THREES, TWOS*
Back hand: four-of-a-kind

Front hand: next two highest cards

Back hand   Front hand

● *FIVE ACES*
Back hand: three Aces

Front hand: two Aces

Back hand   Front hand

APPLYING STRATEGY

When you understand that it is to your benefit to be the dealer/banker, you will pursue games that permit you to become the dealer/banker as frequently as possible. Some casinos will let the same player bank two games in a row. Others will let you bank two out of three. Others may not allow you to be the dealer/banker more than once in every seven hands. Since it is essential for your success to serve as the dealer/banker, you should seek out those casinos or tables where you are permitted to be the dealer/banker as often a possible.

It's also recommended that you circulate among the tables and try to find one where most of the players are passing the dealer/banker position. But don't let anyone know that you're looking for this advantage or you'll be playing by yourself before long.

There are other factors in pai gow poker that must be considered. Casinos can establish rules for setting the casino dealer's hands that are considered aggressive or passive. Aggressive setting of hands makes it more difficult to win, but passive setting may play into the hands of the other players who serve as dealer/banker. As the dealer/banker, you also must be aware of the level of bets. When the other players act as the dealer/banker, you must be aware of how aggressively they set their hands.

Pai gow poker is a favorable game for the casino player, but it is extremely complicated. However, it is not a very volatile game, which means that you can learn while playing with a reasonable chance of winning. Since a substantial proportion of the hands end up in a push, you can play for a long time without losing your bankroll. After getting your feet wet with one of the big five games, you should give pai gow poker a try.

POKER, ISLAND STYLE

One game that has become increasingly popular is Caribbean Stud. As the name implies, the game got its start in the Islands, where inferior blackjack and craps games are the rule. So it didn't seem so unusual that a poker-style game with a prohibitive house advantage would catch on.

What is unusual, is that the game would become popular in Las Vegas and Atlantic City. For some reason, it has.

Even by playing the painfully simple basic strategy, Caribbean Stud still has a rather stiff house advantage of 4.4 percent. And that's if you play perfectly. If you're like most players, who fly by the seat of their pants, you'll be bucking a house edge between eight and 12 percent.

The game is rather simple, and based on poker. After placing their bets, the "ante", the players are each dealt five cards. The dealer also deals himself five cards, but only one, the last, is dealt face up. At this point, the players have two choices. They can play out the hand they were dealt, or they can surrender and give up their antes. Should they decide to play out their hands, they place a bet in the betting circle that is twice as much as their antes. After the players make their decisions, the dealer turns over his remaining cards and makes the best possible poker hand out of his five cards.

But if the dealer doesn't "qualify" with at least an Ace-King, the game is not fully completed. If he fails to have such a hand, every player who has not surrendered gets paid on their ante, but not on the second bet. If the dealer qualifies with an Ace-King or better, he acts on the individual hands. If your hand beats the dealer, you get paid on both bets. The ante bet is paid even money and the second bet is paid off at the particular odds offered at that casino. If the dealer beats your hand, you lose both bets.

CARIBBEAN STUD PAYOFF ODDS

HAND	PAYOFF
Pair or less	*1-1*
Two pair	*2-1*
Three-of-a-kind	*3-1*
Straight	*4-1*
Flush	*5-1*
Full house	*7-1*
Four-of-a-kind	*20-1*
Straight flush	*50-1*
Royal flush	*100-1*
(Odds can vary from casino to casino)	

The problem with Caribbean Stud, from a player's

standpoint, is the requirement that the dealer have an Ace-King. Many players have been frustrated by being dealt a great hand, and have the dealer not qualify. Instead of getting the odds payoff, you only get one-to-one payout on the ante. It's terribly aggravating.

The popularity of Caribbean Stud could be traced to the progressive bet. For a $1 on each hand, you become eligible to win a progressive jackpot by drawing a royal flush and winning the top prize which generally exceeds $100,000. The odds against hitting a royal flush at Caribbean Stud are 649,000-1, so, to say the least, it's a long shot.

To make the progressive bet more palatable, however, the makers of the game added a couple of other payouts that sweeten the pot.

CARIBBEAN STUD PROGRESSIVE JACKPOTS PAYOFFS

HAND	PAYOFF
Pair or less	*none*
Two pair	*none*
Three-of-a-kind	*none*
Straight	*none*
Flush	*$50*
Full house	*$75*
Four-of-a-kind	*$100*
Straight flush	*10% of jackpot*
Royal flush	*jackpot*

Caribbean Stud has spread far beyond the Islands, unfortunately. It can now be found in almost all American casino jurisdictions, along with the Islands and on cruise ships. The company that markets the game estimates that over 600 tables are currently operating, including tables in Europe and Australia.

If you must play Caribbean Stud, do so at your own risk. But at least use the following basic strategy:
● Do not bet the progressive wager unless the jackpot exceeds $150,000.
● Bet every pair or more.
● Bet Ace-King or better (if your hand contains the dealer's upcard).

That's it. It's a simple game, but a poor one.

RIDING THE WAVE

Another poker-style game that has made its mark in the casino world is Let It Ride. While it's house advantage is marginally better for the player than Caribbean Stud, it's still a game that carries a heavy edge for the casino.

Let It Ride is different from Caribbean Stud, and most other poker games. Players don't have to beat a dealer's hand or the other players. They merely have to compile a winning poker hand. In this aspect, Let It Ride is more like video poker than any table game.

The blackjack-sized table contains three betting circles. The player puts three equal sized bets in each circle. In the first round, the players are dealt three cards, and the dealer places two community cards in the center of the table. The player examines his three cards, and if he doesn't like his chances, he can remove one bet. If he likes his chances, he can "let it ride".

The second round of betting gives each player one more card, and the first community card is revealed. The player examines his four-card hand, and makes a decision on the second bet: scratch or let it ride.

If the player scratches, he gets his second bet back, and stays in the game with one more bet in action. Players letting their second bet ride are in the game for two or three bets, depending upon what they did with the first bet.

Players must let the final bet ride. The dealer hands a fifth card to each player and reveals the second community card. The players now make their best five-card poker hand from the five cards in their hands and the two community cards.

The game is gaining popularity in the same way Caribbean Stud has, and, in some cases, is supplanting Caribbean Stud. But in most casinos, there is room for both games.

The even-money payoff on the Tens or better, the ability to withdraw two-thirds of your initial bet, and the fact that the player has only to build a winning hand, and not beat a dealer, are all popular features of Let It Ride.

Bets are paid off according to the following table:

LET IT RIDE PAYOFFS

HAND	PAYOFF
Pair of Tens or more	*1-1*
Two pair	*2-1*
Three-of-a-kind	*3-1*
Straight	*5-1*
Flush	*8-1*
Full house	*11-1*
Four-of-a-kind	*50-1*
Straight flush	*200-1*
Royal flush	*1,000-1*

Shuffle Master Gaming, the developer of Let It Ride, has also developed a tournament format that it uses in Nevada.

Winners of tournaments located in individual casinos advance to the finals, where the grand prize winner can walk off with $2 million.

Let It Ride is an inventive game, and the tournament aspect can be a very interesting sideline for anyone who feels the need to play this appealing game.

DOUBLE DOWN DEAD

The worst of the "new" poker games is Double Down Stud.

DOUBLE DOWN STUD PAYOFFS

HAND	PAYOFF
Pair of Sixes or better	*push*
Pair of Jacks or better	*1-1*
Two pair	*2-1*
Three-of-a-kind	*3-1*
Straight	*5-1*
Flush	*8-1*
Full house	*11-1*
Four-of-a-kind	*50-1*
Straight flush	*200-1*
Royal flush	*2,000-1*

There are two versions of this game—a table game and a video game. You should avoid both because the house edge on the game has been estimated between 12 and 21 percent, depending upon the play.

Once again, the game is played at a blackjack-sized table with two betting areas for each player—"bet" and "double down". Each round is dealt from a newly shuffled deck. Each player is dealt one card face up. The dealer then deals three community cards face up and one face down. At this point all players are given the chance to double their bets. After deciding whether to double their bets, the dealer exposes the final down card, and the hands are paid off according to the following table:

Please don't play this game. But if you must, never double down. Exposing your initial bet to the horrendous house advantage is bad enough, but putting more money out there is insane.

POKER LITE

New casino games that are simply variations of poker are like the proverbial "dime a dozen". While some have attained popularity, such as Caribbean Stud and Let It Ride, others have either been too complicated or had a prohibitive house edge.

Three Card Poker was developed by Derek Webb, an academically-minded gambler from Britain. He looked at the development of the new poker games and compared them to other games that actually predate the American poker tradition. Webb considered such "primitive" games as the British game "brag", "flush" from India and the American game, "guts" which is actually an ancestor of the poker games we know today.

What those games had in common is that they used fewer cards than today's games. Webb developed a new table game that would be simple to understand, offer attractive payouts and give the casinos more action per hour.

Webb introduced the game at two casinos, one in Dublin during March 1995 and the other on the Isle of Man. Response was very positive. As a result, Webb was encouraged to approach the American market, with several Las Vegas and Atlantic City casinos agreeing to test the game.

The Three Card Poker player has the opportunity to make three bets—the ante, in which he competes against the dealer; the Pair Plus bet, in which he is rewarded for a high hand; the Play bet, which is a bonus that gives the player an extra payout for premium hands.

As the name implies, in Three Card Poker, the player and the dealer only use three cards. The game is easy to understand because it uses fewer cards than regular poker.

The strategy is simplified because there are no drawing cards. If the player gets high hands, ranging from a pair to a straight flush, he receives a bonus payout that increases as the hands improve.

The bonus hands give the players three ways to win, but the player does not have to have a premium hand, because he will be paid even money if he beats the dealer's hand.

If the dealer does not have a Queen high hand, players are paid on the ante, the Play and the Pair Plus bets. This gives a high frequency of contested hands, providing excitement for players, whether they are low-stakes players or high rollers.

THREE CARD POKER PAYOUTS	
Ante	1-1
Play	1-1
Tie	Push

PAIR PLUS	
Pair	1-1
Flush	4-1
Straight	6-1
Three-of-a-Kind	30-1
Straight Flush	40-1

ANTE BONUS	
Straight	1-1
Three-of-a-Kind	4-1
Straight Flush	5-1

Most attractive is a reasonable house edge of two percent on the ante bets and 2.3 percent on the Pair Plus bets.

Webb is confident that Three Card Poker will be a success in US casinos, and expects that many other casinos will introduce the game to their gaming mix when the tests are completed in the participating jurisdictions.

DEAD DOG

You can generally tell whether a new game is player-friendly by how long it remains popular. The above games that force the players to buck an unreasonable casino advantage might be popular for a while, but as more and more players lose more often than they win, they'll stop playing. Double Down Stud is already disappearing, and the others that don't give players a fair shot will probably soon follow.

Red dog, a game that was introduced into Nevada in the Eighties lasted a while, until the players got wise to the terrible house edge, and it soon faded away. Inexplicably, Atlantic City casinos received permission to install the game, and before long, the game faded from the tables of the Boardwalk, where any new game was welcome at that time. But because you may run across it in your casino travels, it deserves a few paragraphs, if only to describe how bad it is.

You may have played this game as a child. It is really just "acey deucy" played in a casino. Played at a blackjack-sized table, red dog has two betting spots—"bet" and "raise".

The player places a bet and the dealer removes two cards from the shoe. The cards are placed face up in the center of the table in the boxes indicated. The player now must decide if he wants to "raise" his bet at house odds. The dealer then reveals a third card. If its value falls between the first two, the player wins his original bet at even money and the raise bet at the odds indicated. Remember, however, that the odds paid aren't the true odds, which is what makes the game such a risk for the player.

The card values in red dog are face value for Two through Ten. Jacks are 11, Queens are 12, Kings are 13 and Aces are 14.

If a dealer has a hand of a Five and a Queen, and draws a Six, Seven, Eight, Nine, Ten, or Jack, the player wins. If any other card is drawn, the player loses. If the dealer deals himself a pair, he automatically deals himself a third card. If the third card is the same, the players are paid off at 11-to-1. If it isn't the same card, the players lose. The true odds on getting a third card with eight decks is 12.8-to-1, so even this payoff falls short of the true odds.

The "spread" is the key to red dog. Once again the payoffs don't represent the true odds, and the only hands where it makes sense to raise are those with spreads of seven or more. And that is the essential basic strategy of red dog. Even if you stick to this, you're still bucking odds of around four percent. Not terrible, but much worse than other casino games. And given the table "hold" percentage—the amount of money retained after all bets are paid—very few players understand the basic strategy of red dog. Why would the tables keep more than 30 percent of all money played if that were the case?

THE GAMES LAB

There are many other games that can be found in a casino, and many more are currently being developed. In almost all cases, these games are "house" games that make it virtually impossible to win. Consider it from the casino executives' standpoint. They are already forced by public demand to offer blackjack, craps, roulette and baccarat. While they do everything they can to make those games more profitable for the casino, there's only so much tinkering they can do before the players go elsewhere for their table game action.

So if they're going to introduce new games, they're going to make sure that those games don't make a shambles of their bottom line. That's why the dependable slot machines are their favorite, and that's why you'll hardly ever see games that offer the player a reasonable chance to win.

THE SYSTEMS APPROACH

A GOOD SPORT

The wide range of games in the casino don't interest Jason. He's a gambler, but Jason doesn't care to take the time to memorize the blackjack basic strategy chart, and forget learning how to count cards. Just the thought of it hurts his head.

Jason understands and even enjoys craps from time to time. The reasonable casino edge and the free odds makes a lot of sense to him, but he just can't stand around one table for too long.

No, Jason prefers to bet on something he really understands and enjoys. Ever since he was a boy, Jason has been a sports fan. Watching the competition between individual athletes or the chemistry of team camaraderie captured his imagination like nothing else.

He wasn't a great athlete himself, but he played enough to understand what it takes to be a professional, so has a healthy respect for anyone who reaches that level.

What really amazed Jason was that he could wager on professional sports and actually profit on his predictions

of the results of sporting events.

The more he learned about sports, the better chance he had of winning. The conditioning of the athletes, the weather conditions, the effect of the home field or court and a thousand other variables go into handicapping, and Jason has mastered most of them.

His favorite time is football season, when college football and the National Football League encompass his weekend. The action of the games combined with the excitement that courses through the sports books is what makes sports betting so important to Jason.

Jason actually moved to Nevada so he could have access to legal sports betting. He is so good at what he does that he can actually supplement his income by studying all the different aspects of sports.

So Jason walks right by all the table games and slot machines when he enters a casino. He'd prefer to make bets on games and contests whose results are determined by the performance of humans, not some obscure theoretical equations.

GLOSSARY

TALKING THE TALK

*A Glossary of casino terms so you won't feel
like you're in a foreign country when you enter a casino.*

21 Another name for blackjack.

action Gaming action as measured by the amount wagered over a period of time.

Ace The highest value card in blackjack and poker; the side of the dice with one spot; a dollar bill.

Aces and Eights In poker, this is the "Dead Man's Hand" because it is reportedly the hand held by Wild Bill Hickok when he was shot.

agent A person who works with a cheat.

aggregate limit The maximum amount paid out at a keno game; usually $50,000.

ante In poker, first bet put up by the players before the cards are dealt.

American wheel A roulette game that includes the 0 and 00 numbers.

any craps A wager at craps that the shooter will roll a total of two, three or 12 on the next roll.

any seven A wager at craps that the shooter will roll a seven on the next roll.

automatic shuffler Machines on blackjack tables, and some of the new poker games played at blackjack-sized tables, that shuffle the cards, providing uninterrupted playing, but no chance to count cards.

back line A bet on the craps layout where the player will wager that the shooter will lose.

back the bet Making a free odds bet at craps.

back in At poker, it is entering the betting after first passing or checking to the raiser.

bank The person covering the bets in any game, usually the casino itself. A row of slot machines.

bank hand The second of the two hands at the baccarat game.

bankroll The amount of money a player brings to the casino to gamble.

bar The banning of certain players from the casino, sometimes used against both cheaters and expert players.

barber pole A stack of chips mixed indiscriminately so the values and colors of chips aren't consistent.

basic strategy A system of playing blackjack that takes advantage of the most favorable rules for the player. Can also describe favorable playing methods at other games.

beat To win money by cheating.

beef A dispute, an argument over the conduct of any casino game.

behind the line Betting free odds. The bet is placed behind the player's pass line bet.

best of it Having an advantage.

bet against the dice To bet that the shooter at craps will lose.

bet with the dice To bet that the shooter at craps will win.

bet blind To bet without seeing your cards.

bevels Dice that have been shaved on the corners to favor certain numbers.

biased wheels Roulette wheels that favor certain sections or numbers due to an imperfection in manufacture or balance.

black action A player who is using black, $100 chips.

Black Book A list of persons excluded from a casino in a particular jurisdiction.

blackjack A natural in the first two cards is an Ace and a ten-value card.

bluff In poker, an attempt to win the pot with an inferior hand.

book To confirm a bet someone wishes to make.

bonus poker A form of Jacks-or-better video poker that offers favorable payoffs on certain fours-of-a-kind.

boxman The person who sits in the center of the craps table supervising the game.

boxcars In craps a roll of 12. Also called a *hobo bet*.

break In blackjack, to go over 21. The same as *bust*.

break down a bet To separate the various chips in a bet prior to paying to ensure accuracy.

brushing Substituting cards or dice into a game.

bull In poker, another name for an Ace.

burn When a blackjack or baccarat dealer discards one or more cards from a freshly shuffled deck.

bust out joint A casino that cheats the players.

buy in The process of purchasing chips prior to play. The amount of chips purchased prior to play.

cage The cashier's section of the casino.

call In poker, to see, or match, a bet with the same amount as the previous bet.

call bet A bet made verbally without any money on the table.

caller In baccarat, the dealer who stands on the opposite side of the table from the chip rack and announces the results of the hands. Also called the *croupier*.

C&E In craps, a one-roll bet that any craps (two, three or 12) or 11 will be rolled.

capping a bet Adding one or more chips to a winning bet after a decision has been made when the dealer's attention is diverted. Also known as *past posting*.

card counting A method of playing in blackjack where the player keeps track of the cards already dealt in order to gain an advantage over the casino with the knowledge of the cards remaining to be dealt.

carousel An area of the slot department that includes several slot machines grouped together, usually of the same type, and sometimes linked with a progressive jackpot.

case bet The last of a player's money being risked in one bet.

casino host A casino executive with the job of catering to high rollers.

casino manager The main executive in charge of the casino for all the shifts.

catch The numbers selected by a keno player that correspond to those selected by the keno machine and posted on the keno board.

centerfield The name given to the nine in craps. The center betting position at a blackjack table with even betting areas.

change person A slot employee who changes currency for coins or tokens.

chasing Betting more money in order to recoup earlier losses.

checks Another name for casino chips.

check rack The tray in front of the dealer that holds the chips.

check racker The second dealer at a roulette game who assists the dealer in making payouts and cleaning up losing bets. Also called a *mucker*.

chop A game in which the decisions aren't consistent, with no one side dominating.

chunk To bet a large amount of chips at one time, often with no regard for denominations.

clapper A piece of leather or plastic at the top of the Big Six wheel that, when stopped in a particular slot, signifies the winner.

clocking Tracking the results of any casino game.

cocked dice A condition at craps when the dice land so they are leaning against some object and not flat on the table.

cold A player enduring a long losing streak. A table, deck of cards or dice that keeps beating the players.

come out The first role at a craps table that determines the point.

commission The percentage the house takes out of winning bets at baccarat or pai gow poker or for buy bets in craps. Usually five percent.

comp Short for "complimentary", a reward for players who are regular customers or "action" players at the casino. Usually, a free room or meals.

counter A blackjack player using card counting techniques.

craps The totals of two, three or 12. When rolled on the come-out roll, causes the shooter to lose.

crap out Throwing a two, three or 12 on the come out roll.

credit line The amount of money the casino is willing to lend to an individual player.

crew Personnel who man a craps or baccarat game.

crimp To bend a card at the corner so it is recognizable the next time it is dealt.

curator In baccarat, the player designated to deal the cards.

cut card A yellow card inserted into the deck that indicates the deck needs to be reshuffled at that point.

cut the deck To divide the deck before dealing, usually done by a player with the cut card.

day shift The casino work shift that usually works from 10am to 6pm.

dead hand In poker, a hand that has been discarded. In blackjack or baccarat, a hand that is declared "dead" because of a dealer's mistake.

dead table A game that is staffed by dealers and open for business, but has no players.

Deuces The Two in a deck of cards or the side of the dice with two spots.

Deuces wild A form of video poker in which all the Deuces are wild cards.

dice boat The tray at the craps table that holds the dice.

discard rack The plastic holder on a blackjack table that holds the cards that have already been played.

dime In the sports book, a $100 bet.

do bet Any bet at the craps table that favors the shooter over the house. Same as the **right** bet.

don't bet Any bet at the craps table that favors the house over the shooter. Same as the **wrong** bet.

double down To make a second bet on a player's hand in blackjack equal to or less than the original bet that gives the player only one more card.

Double Exposure blackjack A blackjack game in which the dealer turns both of his cards up. Also known as See-Thru blackjack and other names.

double odds The option of making free odds twice as much as a player's line bet.

draw In video poker, to receive new cards. In blackjack or baccarat to call for more cards.

drop The amount of the total money and markers wagered at a gaming table.

drop box The area of any gaming table where the cash is deposited, usually under the table. It can only be opened in the count room of the casino.

dumping When a dealer is losing consistently and the players are winning a substantial amount of money.

early surrender An option at blackjack where the player could forfeit half his bet even if the dealer had a blackjack.

easy way In craps, the numbers four, six, eight and ten make without doubles.

edge The advantage enjoyed mostly by the casino, but occasionally by the players.

en prison A French option in roulette when a 0 appears, where an even-money bet is held over to the next roll, rather than lost.

even up A bet that has no mathematical advantage for either side.

even money A bet that pays off at 1-to-1.

exposed card A card accidentally turned over during the course of play.

eye-in-the-sky The cameras stationed above every gaming area in every casino and connected to a surveillance room.

face cards The King, Queen and Jack. Also known as **picture** cards.

false cut A cut of a deck of cards that leaves the cards in the same order.

first base The seat to the dealer's immediate left, the first to receive the cards.

flat bet A bet that is paid off at even money. A player who bets the same amount every wager.

floater When the roulette ball gets hung up in the wheel, slowly revolving without dropping.

floating paddle When the casino has collected so much cash that the paddle used to push the cash into the drop box won't go down all the way.

floorman A supervisor in the casino.

fold In poker, to drop out of play.

four-flush Four cards to a flush in poker.

four-of-a-kind Four cards of the same value.

free odds A wager on the point in craps that can be made by anybody with a point bet and that is paid at true odds.

French wheel A roulette wheel with only one 0, not 00.

freeze out To refuse to take bets and force a gambler out of a game.

front line The space on a craps table where players can make a bet that the shooter will make his point. The same as the **pass line**.

full house A hand consisting of three cards of identical ranking and a pair.

full odds The maximum amount of free odds allowed at the craps table.

fun book A coupon book used by casinos to attract customers to their properties.

gaffed Rigged gaming equipment.

gambling stake The amount of money reserved for gambling. Same as bankroll.

George A good tipper.

ghost A stop on a slot machine reel that is blank.

graveyard shift The work shift in a casino that generally labors from 2am to 10am.

greens Chips valued at $25.

grifter A scam or con man.

grind Small money bettor. A gambling system that requires long play for small rewards.

grind joint Casinos that cater to the small money bettors.

hard hand In blackjack, any hand that does not contain an Ace counted as 11.

hard way In craps, a total of four, six, eight, or ten using only pairs.

head-to-head To play against the dealer with no other players. Sometimes called **heads up**.

heat Surveillance by a casino of a suspected card counter or a cheater. Also pressure on a card counter to leave.

heel a bet Putting bets in the same square and off-setting the chips to reveal the chips underneath. Sometimes indicates two separate bets, other times used to reveal higher denomination chips under a stack.

high card A Jack or better.

high hand One of two hands in pai gow or pai gow poker.

high roller A high-stakes gambler.

hit To receive an additional card in blackjack.

hold The amount of money retained by the casino after all bets are paid.

hold'em A form of poker.

hole card The second card of the dealer's hand which he deals to himself face down.

hot A player experiencing a winning streak. Can also refer to cards, dice or a table where the players are winning.

house edge The mathematical advantage the casino enjoys on every game and wager. Also known as the **PC**.

house odds The ratio at which a casino pays off a winning bet. Odds are set by the casino.

house dealer An employee who is only concerned about the casino's bottom line, or one who enjoys seeing people lose.

hustler A cheat who tries to coax money out of unsuspecting players.

inside straight A hand that can be made only by drawing one card. For instance, drawing a Six to a hand of Four, Five, Seven, Eight.

insurance A side wager at blackjack made when the dealer shows an Ace in which the player bets that the dealer is holding a natural blackjack.

156

jackpot A large payout, either on a table or a machine.

joint A derogatory term for a casino.

Joker's wild A form of video poker that uses an extra card (the Joker) as a wild card.

juice The commission that the house charges on buy bets at craps, and winning bank bets in baccarat. Also called *vig* or *vigorish*. The influence that casino executives pass out to lower ranking employees for promotions or special favors.

junket A trip arranged and paid for by a casino for a group of special players.

junket rep The organizer of the junket.

keno board The electronic sign that indicates the winning keno numbers.

keno counter The area where the keno tickets are collected and the winning bets paid.

keno runner An employee who circulates through a casino hotel taking keno bets.

keno writer An employee who works at the keno counter taking bets and paying winners.

kicker In poker, an extra card that is kept with a pair to give the impression that the player has more than simply a pair.

lace In baccarat, a method of mixing the cards after shuffling.

ladder man The casino supervisor who watches a baccarat game from a high chair.

lammers Plastic buttons that signify the amount of commission owed by players at a baccarat game. Also identifies the amount of money issued to a player for a marker.

laying odds For the wrong bettor to make an odds bet on a don't come or don't pass bet.

layout The design imprinted on the table showing the various bets at the games.

Little Joe In craps, a roll of a four. Originates from "Little Joe from Kokomo".

loose machine A slot machine that has been set to return a high percentage of the money played in that machine.

long term The concept that the casino will always win over an extended period of time, and why a player can

win in the short run.

low hand One of the two hands in pai gow and pai gow poker.

low pair In poker, a pair that can't open the betting. In video poker, a non-winning pair.

mark An individual who has been or might be a target to be cheated.

marker A check the player fills out before receiving casino credit at a table. Essentially an IOU.

match play A casino promotion where the player receives a coupon or a non-redeemable chip that can be bet with real money. If it wins, it's paid off with real chips.

mini-baccarat A smaller version of the big baccarat game played for lower stakes.

money plays An expression used in Nevada when the player doesn't want the dealer to exchange his money for chips. A winning bet, however, will be paid in chips.

money wheel Another name for the Big Six wheel.

money management A system that a player uses to conserve his bankroll over the course of his casino visit.

monkey A Ten or a face card.

monster roll A period of time where many points are made and many numbers are rolled. The goal of most craps players.

mucker An individual who uses sleight of hand techniques to cheat. Also, the second dealer at a roulette table.

multiple coin machine Slot and video poker machines that require more than one coin for the top jackpot.

multiple deck games Blackjack games that use two or more decks of cards.

multiple hands To play more than one hand at blackjack.

nail To catch someone cheating.

natural A perfect hand. At blackjack, an Ace and ten-value card. At baccarat, a total of eight or nine in the first two cards. At craps, a seven or 11 on the come out roll.

negative progression Any betting system where you

increase your bets after a loss.

nickel A $5 chip or a $500 bet at the sports book.

no action A term used by a dealer to indicate that the casino will not take a particular bet or that a roll doesn't count.

nut The amount of money the casino needs to make a profit, or the amount of money a player needs to accomplish his goals.

off To remove a bet at craps for one or more rolls. It means no decisions can be made on those bets. Only place and odds bets can be called "off".

on A craps call that your bets are working for the next roll.

one-armed bandits A term given to slot machines.

one-roll bets Any bet that is decided by the very next roll.

on the square A fair and honest game.

open In poker, to make the first bet.

openers Cards that qualify a player to open in poker.

paddle The device used to push money into the drop box.

paint A face card.

pair Two cards of the same value.

palm To conceal money or chips in your palm.

parlay To double a bet after a win.

pass A win by the shooter at craps, either by rolling a seven or 11 on the come-out roll or making the point before rolling a seven.

pat hand Any hand in a card game that requires no additional cards.

pay line The line upon which the payouts depend at a slot machine.

pay the board When a decision is made to pay all the players at a table, usually after a dispute.

penetration The depth a dealer goes into a deck before reshuffling at blackjack.

penny ante A small stakes game.

pit An area containing a number of gaming tables.

pit boss The executive in charge of the pit.

player hand The first of the two hands dealt at baccarat.

plus-minus system The most basic form of blackjack card counting systems.

point The total—four, five, six, eight, nine, or ten—rolled on the come-out roll in craps. The shooter must make this number a second time before rolling a seven to win.

pot The total amount of money at stake on a hand.

pot limit The betting limit is limited to the size of the pot.

power of the pen A casino executive with the authority to grant complimentaries has this power.

premium player Politically correct reference to a high roller.

press To increase the size of a wager after it has won once.

price The house advantage on a given bet.

producer A player who loses heavily and consistently.

progressive jackpot The grand prize offered on certain kinds of linked slot machines. It grows until it is hit by a player.

progressive slots A group of slot machines which have no set maximum jackpot, that grows each time a player makes a bet.

proposition bet Bets in the center of the craps layout. Any bet that carries a high house advantage and is a true longshot.

push A tie.

quarters Green $25 chips.

rail The high padded walls on the craps table. Also the low wall or railing surrounding the baccarat pit.

rail bird A thief who sneaks chips from in front of players on the craps table.

raise To increase the amount of a previous bet at poker.

rake The commission a poker room charges on each pot in a poker game.

rating The evaluation of a player gambling action.

rating card The device used to rate a player.

reds $5 casino chips.

reels One of the loops inside the slot machine that spin around.

reels strips The series of symbols wrapped around a cylinder inside a slot machine that designate a winner.

reel window The glass display through which the players view the reels.

respin When the clapper on the Big Six wheel gets hung

up and doesn't land clearly on one number.

RFB Privileges that allow premium players to receive room, food and beverage.

rich deck When the remaining cards in the deck are favorable to the player at a blackjack game.

roll the bones Shoot the dice.

royal flush A Ten, Jack, Queen, King and Ace of the same suit.

run the shoe When a baccarat player maintains control of the shoe by winning a series of banker bets until all the cards have been dealt.

ruin Losing your entire bankroll.

rush A quick winning streak.

scared money Money a player can't afford to lose.

section shooter A roulette dealer who tries to hit certain areas of the wheel.

section slicing Dividing a roulette wheel into sections to discover if any section is hitting more than others.

send it in Making a large wager.

seven out When a shooter at craps loses by rolling a seven before repeating his point.

shaker The container holding the dice at pai gow, sic bo or pai gow poker.

shield The glass around the roulette wheel that prevents customers from touching the wheel.

shift boss The casino executive in charge of the casino for a designated shift.

shill A casino employee who poses as a player in order to get more players involved at a dead or a slow table.

shoe The box that hold the cards in various games.

shoot To roll the dice.

shooter The person who rolls the dice.

short odds Receiving less than the true payout of the bet.

short term The theory that since the casino has the advantage over the long run, the player can win in short gambling sessions.

showdown In poker, the final betting followed by the comparison of the hands of the remaining players.

shuffle up A tactic aimed at thwarting card counters where the dealer will shuffle as often as every hand.

side bet A second bet, in addition to the primary bet, on a proposition at a table game.

side pot A group of bets at poker in addition to the main pot.

single-deck blackjack A blackjack game that uses only one deck.

sleeper A bet at the craps table that the player has forgotten about or even left the table without collecting.

slot floor The area of the casino where the slot machines are located.

slot mix The designation of the mixture of loose and tight machines, different denominations, and slot machines versus video gaming machines.

slug A group of cards inserted into a blackjack deck that has been arranged in an order known to a dishonest player. Also a piece of round metal that when inserted in a slot machine imitates a coin.

snake eyes The total of two on the craps table.

snapper Slang for a natural blackjack.

soft hand A blackjack hand in which an Ace is counted as one.

split To divide one hand with two identical cards into two hands at the blackjack table.

spooking The skill of discovering the dealer's hole card in blackjack. A spook is player who gets that information and relays it to compatriots.

spread The difference between the minimum and maximum bets of a player.

stack A group of 20 chips, especially with special roulette chips.

stacked deck A deck whose cards have been prearranged.

stand To decline any additional cards at the blackjack table.

steaming A gambler playing recklessly in order to recoup his losses.

stick The device used at the craps table to move the dice around the table. Also called a cane.

stickman The dealer who announces the rolls at the craps table and passes the dice to the shooter.

stiff A blackjack hand that might break if you take a hit, but isn't good enough to be a pat hand. A player who doesn't tip the cocktail waitress or dealer.

stops The number of points where a slot machine reel might become motionless.

straight Five cards in sequence.

straight flush Five cards in sequence in suit.

straight slots Slot machines that have payouts that are set and unchanging.

stuck To lose or to be losing money to the house.

surrender An option at blackjack where the player can give up half his bet before drawing any cards.

sweat A casino executive or player who worries about losing.

swing shift A casino work shift that generally runs from 6pm to 2am.

system A way to gamble that will help the gambler succeed.

take down To recall a wager before a decision is made.

taking odds Taking free odds behind the pass line or a come bet.

tapped out Losing all your money.

tell An unconscious signal that a blackjack dealer communicates to players about the value of his hole card. In poker, an inadvertent signal that allows other players to know what your hand is.

three flush Three cards to a flush.

three-of-a-kind A hand that has three cards of the same value.

third base The position farthest to the right of the dealer. The last player to act on his hand before the dealer.

tight machine A slot machine that returns a low percentage of the money played on that machine.

toke A tip or gratuity.

toke hustler A dealer, waiter or waitress who aggressively encourages players to tip.

Tom Casino slang for a poor tipper.

triple odds Free odds of three times the amount of the player's pass line or come bets.

true odds The actual likelihood of any event happening.

two pair A hand consisting of two separate pairs.

underground joint An illegal casino.

up card The first card of a blackjack dealer's hand.

vic Casino slang for sucker, or victim.

video keno An electronic slot machine that mimics a live keno game. A keno card appears on the screen, and the player picks ten numbers. The machine's random number generator then picks 20 numbers.

video blackjack An electronic slot machine that mimics a live blackjack game.

video poker An electronic slot machine that plays a game similar to live poker, but with significant differences.

video slots An electronic slot machine that is identical to "reel" slot machines, except that the screen reproduces the reels.

vig or vigorish The five percent commission that the casino charges for various casino bets; the same as **juice**.

wager Another term for bet.

wash A situation where one bet cancels out another. Also when dealers spread the cards out on the table prior to shuffling and mixing them face down, sometimes called a pizza.

welch Failing to pay a bet.

wheel The casino term for roulette.

wheel chips The special chips used only at the roulette tables.

wheel head The revolving portion of the roulette wheel.

whip shot A controlled roll of the dice where the dice land flat and do not spin, leaving the two desired sides face up.

wild card A card that can be used for any other in a card game.

wired A hand consisting of a pair with one card face up and one card in the hole.

working Any bet that is in action, but has yet to be decided.

worst of it Being at a disadvantage.

wrong bet Any bet at craps that favors the house over the shooter; the same as a don't bet.

yard A $100 bill.

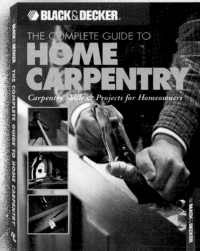
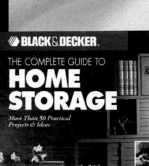
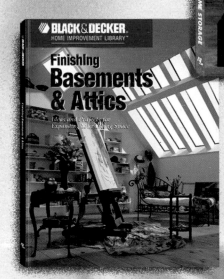

Specialty Workspaces

Laundry and Mud Rooms

Arts, Crafts and Hobbies

page 87:
lamp by
Daylight Company, LLC
Service Center
116 King Court Industrial Park
PO Box 422
New Holland, PA 17557-0422
1-866-DAYLIGHT (329-5444)
www.us.daylightcompany.com

page 90:
cabinets by
Merillat Industries
5353 West US 223
Adrian, MI 49221
To request a catalog or
find a store near you visit
www.merillat.com

page 91:
*Design*Wise tips contributed
by Rosemary McMonigal, AIA
McMonigal Architects
Minneapolis, MN
612-331-1244

page 97:
garden window by
**JELD-WEN® Windows
and Doors**
401 Harbor Isles Blvd.
Klamath Falls, OR 97601
To request a catalog or
find a store near you,
call 1-800-535-3936
or visit www.jeld-wen.com

Relaxation

page 106:   *Design*Wise tips contributed by Tim Quigley, AIA
Quigley Architects
Minneapolis, MN
612-692-8850

page 109:   design by
Quigley Architects
Minneapolis, MN
612-692-8850

page 111:   design, furnishings, and accessories by **IKEA**
To shop, request a catalog, or find a store near you, call
1-800-434-4532
or visit www.IKEA.com

page 112-113:   design, furnishings, and accessories by **IKEA**
To shop, request a catalog, or find a store near you, call
1-800-434-4532
or visit www.IKEA.com

page 116 (below):   cabinets by
Plato Woodwork, Inc.
Plato, MN 55370
For more information, call
1-800-328-5924 or visit
www.platowoodworking.com

page 118-119:   design, furnishings, and accessories by **IKEA**
To shop, request a catalog, or find a store near you, call
1-800-434-4532
or visit www.IKEA.com

page 120 (above):   Design by
Quigley Architects
Minneapolis, MN
612-692-8850

page 121:	design, furnishings, and accessories by **IKEA** To shop, request a catalog, or find a store near you, call 1-800-434-4532 or visit www.IKEA.com
page 122:	design, furnishings, and accessories by **IKEA** To shop, request a catalog, or find a store near you, call 1-800-434-4532 or visit www.IKEA.com
page 125:	egress window and scapeWEL Window Well by **The Bilco Company** P.O. Box 1203 New Haven CT 06505 www.bilco.com
page 126-127 (both):	sauna by **Finnleo Sauna & Steam** Cokato, MN for more information call 1-800-FINNLEO or visit www.finnleo.com

Additional Resources

INTERNATIONAL CODE COUNCIL (ICC)

www.iccsafe.org
The International Code Council (ICC) was established in 1994 as a nonprofit organization dedicated to developing a single set of national construction codes in the following areas: Building, plumbing, fire, mechanical, energy conservation, zoning, electrical, and others. They also offer the following services:
- Code application assistance
- Educational programs
- Certification programs
- Technical handbooks and workbooks
- Plan reviews
- Automated products
- Monthly magazines and newsletters
- Publication of proposed code changes
- Training and informational videos
- Consumer and safety tips

ICC OFFICES

Headquarters
5203 Leesburg Pike, Suite 600
Falls Church, VA 22041
703-931-4533

Birmingham District Office
900 Montclair Rd.
Birmingham, AL 35213
205-591-1853

Chicago District Office
4051 W. Flossmoor Rd.
Country Club Hills, IL 60478
1-800-214-4321

Los Angeles District Office
5360 Workman Mill Rd.
Whittier, CA 90601
1-800-284-4406

ICC SUBSIDIARIES

ICC Evaluation Service Business/Regional Office
5360 Workman Mill Rd.
Whittier, CA 90601
562-699-0543

Regional Office
900 Montclair Rd., Suite A
Birmingham, AL 35213
205-599-9800

Regional Office
4051 West Flossmoor Rd.
Country Club Hills, IL 60478
708-799-2305

International Accreditation Service
5360 Workman Mill Rd.
Whittier, CA 90601
562-699-0541

International Code Council Foundation
PO Box 11335
Cincinnati, OH 45211
513-574-0957

CONSUMER REPORTS

Customer Relations Department
101 Truman Ave.
Yonkers, NY 10703
www.consumerreports.org

www.consumerreports.org is the place to go if you're contemplating an appliance, computer, or electronics purchase.
www.consumerreports.org is an independent nonprofit organization whose mission is to work for a fair, just, and safe marketplace for all consumers and to empower consumers to protect themselves. They perform expert testing on thousands of products in the following categories:

Appliances
Refrigerators, washers, dishwashers, dryers, vacuum cleaners.

Electronics & computers
Cell phones, digital cameras, TVs, PDAs, laptops, camcorders.

Home & garden
Air conditioners, grills, deck treatments, lawn mowers & tractors.

Health & fitness
Exercise & diet, treadmills, dangerous supplements.

NATIONAL ASSOCIATION OF HOME BUILDERS (NAHB)

1201 15th St., NW
Washington, DC 20005-2800
1-800-368-5242
www.nahb.org

The National Association of Home Builders is an excellent resource for information, education, research, technical expertise, economic and housing data, codes & standards, and finding remodelers/builders in your area.

OTHER RESOURCES

Black & Decker®
The Complete Guide to Home Carpentry: Carpentry Skills & Projects for the Homeowner

Black & Decker®
The Complete Guide to Home Storage: More Than 50 Practical Projects & Ideas

Black & Decker®
The Complete Guide to Windows & Doors: Step-by-Step Projects for Adding, Replacing & Repairing All Types of Windows and Doors

Black & Decker®
The Complete Guide to Easy Woodworking Projects: 50 Projects & Ideas

Photo Credits

Index